P9-CMK-021

THOSE DISTURBING MIRACLES

1217

BY

LLOYD C. DOUGLAS

Author of
"The Minister's Everyday Life"
"These Sayings of Mine"

2 2 6.7
D 73T

HARPER & BROTHERS *Publishers*
New York *and* London

1 9 2 7

LINCOLN PUBLIC LIBRARY
LINCOLN, ILLINOIS

MADE AND PRINTED IN THE
U. S. A. COPYRIGHT, 1927, BY
HARPER & BROTHERS
FIRST EDITION
H-B

Contents

35506

67823

LINCOLN PUBLIC LIBRARY
LINCOLN, ILLINOIS

Foreword

SO abundant is the present output of reflective literature that every thoughtful reader owes it to himself to be almost meticulous in his selection of speculative books.

Occasionally a speculative book may have good reasons for being equally discriminating in its choice of
readers.

This book is intended for persons who are disturbed
about the miraculous element in the Christian religion;
for those who, while deeply revering the Bible as an
unsurpassed record of a great race's spiritual evolution, are not prepared to accept its stories of magical
deeds; for those who, while recognizing the moral
grandeur and unerring wisdom of Jesus, wish they
might consider themselves his followers without being
required to believe in him as a magician.

Not only does this book decline to solicit any other
patronage than that indicated above, but hereby offers a
friendly caution to at least two distinct types of potential readers who may do themselves a disservice by
venturing further into this study. The caution is not
shouted in such a mood of testy inhospitality as obviously inspires the shrill placard, "KEEP OUT! THIS
MEANS YOU!" It is extended cordially, hoping to
reduce the risk of foisting upon an unsuspecting pur-
chaser something he will later deem a bad bargain.

Whoever considers the miracle stories of the Bible
—more particularly the records of strange deeds predi-

cated of Jesus—as merely absurd and undeserving of intellectual respect, will find so little of interest here that he is advised to save the price of the book.

Whoever is entirely at peace in regard to this matter, satisfied to accept the miracles as they stand, with an uninquiring faith in their literal truth, is urgently requested to let well enough alone, for exactly the same reason that healthy people should never sample medicines intended for the sick. The injunction served against this type of mind, warning it away from the pages which are to follow, is not a mere economic measure proposed to save somebody's money, but his peace of mind, a consideration vastly more important.

Now that there has been a sufficient display of candor in our attempt to restrict this book's clientele to the class of people for whom it is written, we will plunge into our task without further preamble, stoutly refusing to be held responsible either for the yawning disinterest of the scoffer or the eloquent discomforts of the credulous. If they are determined to proceed, in the face of the warnings we have posted, they do so at their own risk.

THOSE DISTURBING MIRACLES

All writing in or marking of books, turning down of leaves, or other defacement are forbidden and punishable by fine.

CHAPTER ONE

THE INFANCY OF GREAT FACTS

I

PRACTICALLY every important fact now blooming in the garden of modern knowledge was evolved from some worthless weed once growing wild in a dense jungle of myth, legend, and superstition.

Chemistry's grandmother, Alchemy, was an old witch who operated a little café in a wayside cave where bat-wing soup and toad-liver marmalade were solemnly served to a miscellaneous constituency ranging in personnel all the way from the king in his royal robes to the pauper in his rotting rags.

Let any man of five senses, however ignorant, be given a fire and a kettle, and turned loose in a meadow to gather herbs, roots, and flowers; let him spend his days brewing and distilling experimental messes, no matter how absurd his motives for doing so—it will be strange indeed if he does not accidentally compound some concoction which proves to be a stimulant, a sedative, a purge, an emetic, or an ointment. If, having made an important discovery, he administers his dose to the accompaniment of mysterious words and grave gestures, he may come to be quite a figure in the esteem of all who enjoy the sensation of being befuddled in the presence of that which they cannot comprehend.

Chemistry has not far to climb, in its family tree, before arriving at an ancestry of whom, if one were to say that it was myth-ridden and quack-harried to the utmost degree, one would be merely saying nothing at all: words fail to express it.

Astronomy's grandfather, Astrology, consulted the stars only to learn how the king's health was going to be next Monday, when he proposed—all signs being favorable—to set forth with his bow and arrows and an armful of smooth stones to wage war upon some neighboring potentate whose I. Q., according to present estimates, probably registered a mental age of about seven years and two months.

The astrologers blinked sedately at the stars, by night, and spent the daytime examining the viscera of slaughtered sheep to see if perchance some portentous tidings, of vast interest to the court, might not be recorded there as impressively as in the firmament. But, let a dozen generations of men spend every night gazing aloft, however ridiculous may be their motive, and it goes without saying that they will discover a few important facts about the movement of the heavenly bodies.

Not to admit our deep indebtedness to the painstaking researches of these old-world seers, and our obligation to them for the crude charts they drew— now of inestimable value in the study of certain remote planets—would be unworthy of any man interested in the advancement of science.

We can make full use of these old sky-maps, however, without feeling obliged to accept all the superstitions which motivated the search of their creators; precisely as we may avail ourselves of the anodynes discovered by the alchemists without embracing the theories they held concerning love potions and elixirs of life. The sky-maps were crowded with pictures of strange animals inhabiting the sidereal territories with which the astrologers were less intimately acquainted. Whoever prefers, today, to accept these charts—animals and all—is guaranteed the right to do so under the laws of our land. Some would make serious use of the maps in so far as they relate to the positions of the stars, and omit the animals from consideration.

Because an important fact of high value to the world was once embedded in superstition, and traduced from age to age on the wings of fantastic myths, does not discredit it. Indeed, the romantic story of its preservation, by this story process, should only add interest to it for every person who appreciates the privileges of modern knowledge.

But to feel ourselves bound to accept the hypotheses of the primitives who, stumbling upon epoch-making discoveries while in quest of other things, explained their findings in terms of a naïve superstition, is to be unfaithful to our present duty to give such energies and elements a better chance to confer benefits upon our world. These things must be kept clearly in mind as we venture upon a study of the miraculous element in religion; for when we consider religion we are dealing with an ancient quest. It was the first of all great facts.

II

It may be assumed that man's earliest speculative thought, after he had mentally developed to the stage of making inquiries about the whence, whither, and primary motive of human existence, was a question relating to his Creator. Because the type of religious thought with which we are concerned sinks its roots into Hebraic lore, it will pay us to make a brief excursion into this ancient literature.

To the best of our information, humanity's original efforts at self-expression were effected in pottery. It is by tracing the early ethnic races backward, through their crude earthenware, that we discover about all that we seem destined to know of them and their manner of life. The ancient Hebrews knew this, perhaps even better than we. Indeed, their own handicraft was limited almost exclusively to the fabrication of earthen utensils.

How natural that they should have pictured their Maker as the Great Potter! Not only is it reasonable that they should have had this conception of Him; it is an idealism beautiful enough to have been worthy

4

of more experienced minds than theirs. When, therefore, we read in the opening pages of the Bible that
one Jehovah shaped the dust of the ground into the
form of a man, and breathed into that dust the breath
of life, surely we were too exacting if we asked for a
better explanation than this at the hands of men who
knew so very little about the world in which they
lived. If we, today, several millennia later, find that
explanation inadequate, and wish to account for man's
origin by some other technique, it may be presumed
that we have as good a right to use our imaginations
as these ancient potters.

The allegation, prominent in these priceless documents of the early Hebrews, that Jehovah on various
occasions said this, that, or some other thing in the
course of hand-to-hand contacts with the leaders of this
self-confessedly "chosen" race, may be taken for whatever it appears to be worth to anyone conversant with
the other holy books of other heaven-questing primitives.

According to these ancient records, Jehovah did not
always conduct Himself as one might expect a God to
act. Of course it is a mere impertinence for any human
being, however wise he thinks himself, to devise an
ideal moral program for Deity, and suggest a code of
right living which He would do well to follow. But
the fact remains that there are two diametrically oppo-
site motives possible for any personality concerned with
this world's affairs—be that personality human or

divine. There is a right motive, rooted in a desire to be constructive and generous, demonstrated to be right by reason of the fact that wherever it is practiced the results are good; and there is a wrong motive, rooted in a passion to be vindictive and destructive, demonstrated to be wrong because its achievements are always and everywhere bad. When, therefore, the ancient Hebrews predicate of their Jehovah certain deeds obviously motivated by vengeance and ill temper, it is merely absurd for us, at the present hour, to invent any frail and fanciful theories to justify such doubtful ethics. More simple and consistent by far is our assumption that the Great Potter, in the esteem of the little potters, was not much better than they were at their very best. They conceived of as great a God as their imagination and ingenuity could devise, but both their imagination and their ingenuity had limitations. All this happened a very long time ago—long before the queer sky-charts of the astrologers, with their wild animals and grotesque monsters sprawling across the parchment.

It requires brains to read the Bible. The idea some people entertain, that this hallowed book should be placed in every human's hand, regardless of his years and intellectual experience, is based upon the erroneous belief that anybody, anywhere, at any age, may be expected to derive magical benefits by reading it, no matter how ignorantly. Quite to the contrary, the child and the untutored adult should be taught only

6

certain easily explained facts set forth by this venerable volume. It is as indefensible to place a copy of the Bible in the hands of early adolescence and expect youth to deduce from it the present imperatives of religion, as to offer a small boy a textbook on geography composed of the world-maps drawn by Anaximander in the year 600 B.C., and the opinions of Aristotle concerning the structure of the earth, and Ptolemy's seven-volume atlas produced in A.D. 150. These ancient efforts to classify and record such knowledge as was possessed long ago, relating to the world's form and configuration, are of intense interest to the trained mind; but this mass of crude and inadequate speculation, arrived at many ages past by men who lacked the proper instruments and data for the correct understanding of problems in the field of geography, should be studied only after one has become fully conversant with the actual facts about the world.

It would be much better for children to become thoroughly trained in the modern conception of Deity and man's apparent relation to Him, spiritually, before being introduced to the Jehovah of the Israelites; for Jehovah, as a moral mentor, leaves a great deal to be desired. Exactly as the astronomers, before the days of the telescopes, thought that the configurations on the surface of the moon were reflections of similar shapes of land and water on the surface of our earth, so did the early Hebrews look up into the face of their Jehovah and see mirrored there the apotheosis of their

7

own gifts, graces, and aspirations, which were frequently lacking in the steadiness of purpose and love-tempered justice at present considered imperative to any right action, human or divine.

In the lore of every ancient people there was a Flood story. Modern science does not doubt the fact of a flood so widespread and devastating that it may have come very near to exterminating the human race. Most of the Flood myths postulate an enraged Deity punishing a wicked world. No singularity is to be ascribed to the Flood legend in our Bible; and whatever stock may be taken in it should be understood as our preference for the Hebrew version over any of the others; the Japanese, for example. Noah's ark is built with a more painstaking nicety of detail than any of the other boats used by ethnic refugees; but all of the lucky fugitives, whether in the Hebrew tale or other tales, are understood to be saved by sufferance to breed a better stock. The stories are nearly enough alike to insure against any one of them honestly claiming the exclusive right to divine authorship, and different enough to forestall any well-founded belief that they might all have proceeded from the pen of God.

The main point at issue in these early explanations of essential facts is this: we may believe that God created man without accepting the legend that Jehovah formed the first human being of the dust of the ground. The primitives were justified in thinking as they did. The dust of the ground was the basic material for creative expression. Dust was the first important fact in human history. It will probably be also the last. The idea is about as idealistic as could be expected of people who knew so little. It is our task to lift the important fact that God is man's Creator out of this legend and assume the right to credit the fact and reject the legend, exactly as astronomy accepts the old sky-charts of the astrologers but merely smiles at the grotesque pictures of their sky animals.

In like mood, we may accept the fact of the flood— whatever benefit that belief may be worth, at this date —without accepting the fanciful tale of a Noah who drove all forms of fauna into his boat, two by two; entered with his household; closed the door; embarked upon his perilous voyage from the valley to the top of a high mountain, leaving behind him all his friends and neighbors, including the frantic parents and brothers and sisters of his sons' wives, now safe and snug in the ark.

We, too, have many problems to solve in dealing with the vast number of moral delinquents who retard the progress of civilization, but we have devised a much better program than wholesale extermination. We do not like to feel that we are so much wiser than God. To avoid that uncomfortable state of mind, we may candidly disbelieve the whole of the Hebrew Flood story, except the bare fact that there was a flood.

Whatever may become of these legends, in our esteem, it is very important that we entertain an atti-

tude of reverence and respect for God. If any legend
—no matter in what book it may be written, or by
whom; let the book be ever so holy, and the writer certain of his heavenly inspiration—predicates of God
certain motives, passions, and aims which we know by
experience and observation are ungenerous and destructive, we are privileged to dissect out of the myth
whatever salient facts seem worth preservation, and
place what is left of the tale in the museum alongside
the stories of Prometheus, Jason, Phœnix, and Ali
Baba.

It may be presumed that many a saintly hand will
be closed into a fist as these words are read. One
greatly prefers not to give the offense that this study is
sure to provoke in the minds of persons wholly committed to a belief in the verbal inspiration of the Scriptures. They were cautioned, however, against coming
in here. So long as they are here, and insist upon being
troubled, let them make what they can of a Jehovah
who orders the thief, Achan, led out to be stoned by
his fellow citizens. It is not sufficient that Achan be
stoned; but his wife, their children, their little flock
of sheep and cattle, all are led out, at the command of
Jehovah, and stoned to death by the community.
Everybody attends to participate in the ghastly murder, according to divine instructions.

Whoever would like to believe in the love and wisdom of an unchanging God, the same yesterday, today,
and forever, will have a great deal of skillful explaining

to do if he hopes to associate the Jehovah of this myth with the Absolute God. One takes one's choice; one keeps the myth and becomes an atheist, or preserves one's faith in and respect for God and abandons the myth. To attempt to keep both requires the surrender of one's mental integrity.

III

At this point it is pertinent to inquire whether there is any ground for belief in divine intervention in human affairs. Shall we be content with a Creator and Conserver of the world, who expects humanity to develop mentally and morally through experience and the increasing utilization of energies latent in our world; or may be see evidences of a divine guidance otherwise expressed than through the natural laws, and the benefits accruing to the race by the development of physical forces: In other words, does God ever speak to men, directing them to seek, in certain places and by suggested processes, for new knowledge which may be productive of good?

The Bible is filled with reports of God's special interventions, revelations, and providential acts. We have found that many of these stories of divine leading are clearly mythical. Is there an element of fact here which must not be disregarded, however little credence may be attached to the legends?

The more we study the history of civilization, the

more we are disposed to believe that God has been opening man's way to the discovery and development of great facts, from the very beginning of human existence. But if Deity ever communicated with men, by way of special revelations, we must insist that such supernal disclosures have not been restricted to any particular era or area.

If God spoke to Abraham, Isaac, and Jacob, when there was nothing more eventful to talk about than the equitable division of herds and the location of greener grazing grounds for a little colony of nomadic shepherds, surely He might, with even larger warrant, speak to our modern world, now in the grip of problems which, as compared with the perplexities of those ancient Bedouins, are as everything is related to nothing.

We are willing that God shall inspire and direct the enactment of the Ten Commandments, but only on condition that He be permitted to authorize and formulate all the great regulating and liberating documents in the history of the race. We are willing that Paul shall see a blinding light and hear an entreating voice on the road to Damascus, but only with the proviso that a misguided leader, today, may also hear and see, unmistakably, that which sets him going triumphantly toward the street called Straight. The whole field of divine revelations must be reinvoiced, relieving it of its time boundaries and racial restrictions and its localized arealities.

The bare fact that Isaac Newton was born on the night that Galileo died is of vastly more interest to the student disposed to seek light on the hypothesis of a special divine guidance, than the story of the succession of the tribal chiefs of the early Hebrews.

Young Michael Faraday, driven by necessity to a humble task in a bookbindery where for weeks he hourly confronts a group of problems in Physics on the sheets he is folding into pages for Ampère's new work on applied electricity; and leaves his gainful occupation for a long grind of lonely starvation while he toils on the manufacture of the first dynamo is more stirring than the story of Moses lured from his sheep trail by the sight of a heaven-ignited mountain shrub.

Gutenberg, sinking a lucrative business into hopeless insolvency, and losing every friend he had, while he experiments for years with the problem of movable types, is a more significant figure than Abraham setting forth toward a promised land, "not knowing whither he went." For these uncanonical disclosures made to other than self-confessedly holy men, of facts and forces imperative to humanity's progress, seem to indicate that God is still actively concerned with the advancement of mankind.

What we want now more than anything else in the field of religion is a clear conception of the nature and process of divine guidance. It is possible that we may find more assistance, at this hour, in a study of this problem, by consulting the physicist rather than the metaphysician. Theology and philosophy have had their innings in the task of defining the relation of God to His world. During our own era, perhaps the most significant disclosures of divine activity in human affairs will be identified with experimental science. This reappraisement of Deity, whereby His Jovian caprice and Jehovistic impetuosity are eliminated in he interest of a steady and law-loving God, apparently eager to disclose great facts to the race as rapidly as human intelligence evolves to the point of utilizing them without too serious risk, is an undertaking now more clearly vested in the keep of the scientist than of the pietist.

Of course, religion has ever been and will continue to be an affair of the heart. Its most rewarding adventures have been motivated by faith, which bases its surest evidences upon things unseen. To leave out of a discussion of religion any recognition of the mystical element is not to be talking about religion at all. No man, however, should ask his faith to carry burdens which his knowledge might bear more naturally if he went to the bother of informing himself concerning his world. No man should load his emotions with traffic more properly consigned to his intellect. There will be plenty of hard work for his faith to do, after his fullest knowledge has proved inadequate; and when he declares that he accepts by faith that which might have been arrived at by knowledge readily accessible, his piety may be mere laziness, and his prompt credulity but a misdemeanor outcropping from an habitual mental immorality.

The research now in demand, relating to the problem of God's leading in our present life, does not involve an indifference to the Bible. In that book is recorded the history of a spiritual progress—at once a pilgrimage and an evolution—experienced during some thirty-five centuries by a race of people uniquely concerned with the quest of God's will for the world, and peculiarly endowed with a talent and temperament for conducting that search consistently. To proceed, today, on an investigation of the will of The Absolute for our lives, without this great book in hand, would be as indefensible as a modern astronomer's study of the sky, disdainful of the charts and journals of his professional forbears.

Recently, however, there has been a curious recrudescence in the public mind to the attitude which Jesus deplored when, addressing the leaders of religious thought, in his own generation, he said, "Ye search the scriptures, thinking that in them ye have eternal life." We, like the Scribes, have been relying too heavily upon the ethical findings of the ancients. An on-coming generation of young men and women, more adequately informed than their parents concerning the world in which they live, are asking the age-old question about God's relation to humanity; and we have mostly contented ourselves by referring them to the

15

Bible, the last page of which was composed nearly two millennia ago, on the other side of the earth.

There is a tang of unintended Deism in this procedure which puts religion too definitely in the pluperfect tense to be of much avail to the modern mind. That ancient Jehovistic religion was evolved mostly by shepherds living the elementary pastoral life of the lonely plains; men who more often than otherwise were politically enslaved, socially restricted by tribal insularities, and intellectually enisled against any broadening contacts with an outside world. This is most assuredly true of the people with whom the Old Testament has to do, and of them by whom it was written; and one may suppose that the New Testament writers, also, were not conversant with the practical endeavors of contemporaneous scholars to make daily life a bit more livable for the average man.

Paul of Tarsus, for example (and it should be remembered that our American brand of Christianity has been and is distinctly Pauline), was so thoroughly committed to his belief that the end of the world would occur in his own lifetime that it was of small concern to him what his contemporaries were doing to add to the welfare and effectiveness of an existence presently to wind up with a mighty crash and a quick judgment. For almost four centuries immediately preceding Paul's era, the social order had been blest with a brilliant galaxy of able thinkers in many fields of research. A group of philosophers had spoken words still held today in high esteem by the academic world. It is almost inconceivable that Paul should not have heard of Plato. One wonders why the Tarsan never makes so much as a cryptic allusion to the great systems of thought elaborately built up by a notable succession of master minds. Aristotle's university, with an endowment and equipment unsurpassed until comparatively recent times, offered courses in palæontology, ethnology, anthropology, and the elementary natural sciences. Nor was that learning to be despised. It was there that the earth was declared a sphere, fully two thousand years before that great fact was experimentally verified; and the globe in use, before the class in geodesy, presented a world differing in measurement from our present computation by a small matter of only sixty-seven miles. To all this Paul was indifferent.

One Marcus T. Cicero wrote, when Paul was a little boy, of the comfort he was finding in his new reading glass which had come to the aid of his aging eyes. In the ruins of Herculaneum, which went out of business during the lifetime of Paul, there was found a microscope with a focal length of nine diameters. But Paul did not know, or, if he knew, did not care, about progress in that field, if we may deduce his lack of information on that subject from his implication that mortal understanding was so frail it was as if one saw through a glass, darkly. In the first century, Hero of Alexander had invented a small turbine engine. It had been known since Theophrastus, four hundred years earlier, that an electric spark could be produced by friction. But Paul knew nothing about such matters; nor did any of the other New Testament writers, if we may estimate the extent of their ignorance of these themes by the eloquence of their silence. They were primarily interested with the affairs of another world than this. And while we revere the consecrated energies they applied to their distinctive task of pointing towards a fairer world, and the technique by which that world might be reached, these holy writings leave practically untouched the whole of man's endeavor to make this world a better place to live in. It is not much wonder, then, if the new generation, today, seeking its own place in the general scheme of things, goes more eagerly and confidently to science for instruction than to the venerable documents bequeathed to them through our organized religion.

IV

The fact should be borne in mind, however, that Science has been making larger claims for itself, in the task of putting the world on its feet, intellectually, than the case justifies. Apparently absent-minded and forgetful of the historic truth that every great fact known to men was cradled in superstition, a certain group of scientists scornfully declare that religion, with its mole-eyed dogmatism, has forever been a ball and chain to the leg of scholarly research. Modern Science would like to leave the impression with its youthful votaries that it has been engaged in a running fight with religion, since the dawn of time.

One might imagine, from the way some scientific men voice this complaint, that on the day Joshua commanded the sun to stand still, a special committee of protest came duly authorized by the International Astronomical Society to plead with Joshua not to do this thing; but Joshua would, anyway, against all their advice. Why did not the astronomers take Joshua around the corner, that afternoon, and say, "General, you're an unqualified success as a fighter and politician, but what you don't know about solar affairs would reach from where you stand to the nethermost suburbs of the Aurora Borealis. You see, the sun does not spin around the earth. Quite to the contrary, the earth revolves around the sun. If you try to do this thing, or let the report get out that you ever thought you could do it, you will only make yourself ridiculous." Why did not the astronomers say the equivalent of that to Joshua? For the very excellent reason that they believed precisely as he did. All that Joshua thought he knew about the sun, he had had from the official stargazers.

Our scientific group, today, is much amused over the story of the crafty Jacob, who, having agreed with his equally slippery father-in-law, Laban, to take as his share of their common flock all the streaked and speckled lambs, tried to stimulate volume production of this species by setting up streaked and speckled poles for the sheep to look at during the breeding season. Of course that's funny. Anybody who cannot laugh heartily at that either has some secret sorrow or flunked in biology. But who is the target for this joke? It is surely not Jacob, who made no pretense of being a biologist. Jacob was a shepherd. Why did not the biologists of the period inform Jacob on the subject of heredity? Why was it that they kept silent and permitted Jacob and all his heirs and assigns and all the rest of the human race, on down to Mendel, to hold precisely this same theory concerning prenatal influences? Was anybody—religion, for example—trying to corner the biologists and herd them toward the inquisitional rack and flame every time they rose up to announce a better hypothesis in the matter of heredity? Not at all; and when the discovery was finally made it did not originate with some persecuted research man whom a squint-eyed Church had harried until his life was endangered, but by the pious abbot of Brunn, in his little laboratory out back of the cloister. Let all the sneering scoffers who loudly inveigh against religion as a drag and incubus to scientific achievement keep it in mind that the present hypothesis employed in all researches in the general field of eugenics was deduced by a man whose laboratory uniform was a long brown cassock, from the girdle of which hung a wooden cross.

It is far from true that the advocates of religion

have always stood waiting with the handcuffs at the open doors of the calaboose to make life unlovely for the research men. The rather dismaying fact is that Science has really settled down to business only in recent years; and it is not very sporting of it to invent, as an alibi for its own tardiness of effort, that it would have been more prompt if religion, with its nauseous superstitions, had not forever blocked the way.

One imagines that the ardent scoffer will find this phase of our study highly displeasing. But he was told on page one to keep out of the book; and now that he is still with us, let him comfort himself with a few cases in point. There are men now living and in good running order who were alive when telegraphy was invented. Telegraphy is a simple application of the first fact ever discovered about electricity. Eighteen centuries elapsed between the original experiment in making and breaking a circuit, and the adaptation of that principle to telegraphy; and not a soul on earth —be he religious or otherwise—was doing anything, meantime, to retard the progress of this idea.

Now and then the doctors tell us, with a sigh, that if they had not run up against the dead wall of religious superstition and pious hocus-pocus every time they wanted to attempt some practical research, they could have done some really wonderful things by now. Let us not have any nonsense about this matter. Our Pilgrim fathers had harvested seven crops of corn in this raw new country before the medical fraternity of the world became aware that the blood circulates in the human body. The clinical thermometer was invented during the time of the Civil War. Anæsthesia was discovered while Thomas Jefferson was President of the United States. The first bathtub erected in this country was inaugurated in 1843, and the next morning's papers carried a warning against it as a menace to health. The resolution was not signed by the Ministerial Association, either. It was signed by the Medical Association.

All great facts have come to us through a long and interesting process of gradual release from superstition. This is true of the facts resident in religious culture, and is as true of the facts imperative to all other cultures, including affairs in the realm of the physical sciences. Whoever hoots at the myths of early religion, and fails to note that every other human interest was in the same predicament, of old, would do himself credit by acquiring some information on the subject which may easily be had at the cost of a few hours' reading.

The truth is that whatever advancement science boasts has been made through researches conducted in buildings erected and through equipment bought and by teachers employed and encouraged by people who not only believed implicitly in the Christian religion, but were for the most part ardent churchmen. Without a single exception, the educational institutions of this country in which the chief scientific progress has been made and from which the greatest scientific declarations have emanated, were founded by Christian ministers, paid for by Christian laymen, and carried to increasing usefulness on the budgets of Christian churches. And had these institutions been required at any time in their lives to look for their support to the little group that derides religion and considers it unimportant to successful living, the sheriff would have tacked a notice on the laboratory door announcing the early public sale of a job lot of test tubes, retorts, and bake ovens.

However, the time has come when the reappraisement of the conception of Deity's dealings with mankind will attach a new responsibility to the endeavors of scholarly research. Test tube and blowpipe will become invested with all the significance once claimed by surplice and chalice. What is to be seen in the fluoroscope will be as important as anything to be seen in a stained window. The Bunsen burner will be as potent as the censer.

It will be the task of this forward-looking movement in religion to learn anew the will of God, who speaks with one tremendous energy through poets' pen and prophets' parchment, through scalpel and forceps, mallet and chisel, dredge and crane, microscope and telescope, dynamo and dynamite, radium and radio, urging humanity to free itself of its physical inhibitions and mental adhesions that it may make a broader quest of life's astounding privileges.

Our generation has been seriously deflected from this search for God's kingdom. Noisy and neurotic, one wing of the public seeks distractions which it hopes will numb its inherent longing for reality. Equally clamorous and psychopathic, another turbulent crew hopes to find, in a backward march toward an obsolete necromancy, some magic formula which will recreate the soul of the generation and incline its heart toward a consideration of the divine.

Disdainful of these appeals, either to find satisfaction in the giddy confusions of artificial joy, or in the frowning fanaticisms of a lugubrious piety, the more thoughtful of the new generation stand troubled, wondering whether a third alternative may be honorably achieved.

Let us renew the ancient quest for knowledge of God's providence, over a road brilliantly lighted by the new scientific discoveries, but paved with the myriad footprints of that host who, without the knowledge, and groping in the fog of superstition, nevertheless helped to make straight the way of and to the Lord.

v

To an adequate understanding of their mood who wrought the ancient writings which contain so much that is incredible, and so much that is of value to anyone interested in the story of humanity's spiritual evolution, it is imperative that we acquaint ourselves with the conditions under which the Hebrew minstrels composed the epics of their race.

Several hundred years before the early annals of the Israelites were reverently and laboriously inscribed by their wise men upon the dried pith of the papyrus plant, an important law was enacted in the higher councils of that nation which had a profound effect upon all their literature. Not to realize the significance of that ordinance is equivalent to making an approach to Jewish lore without the one fundamental fact in hand which accounts for the motive and technique of its writers.

The longest Commandment of the ten essential statutes formulated by Moses involved a sweeping inhibition against any form of pictorial or graphic art. That this drastic injunction was intended to prevent the Hebrews from idolatry in no way alters the fact that it effectually stifled any attempt on the part of these highly idealistic people to project their imagery otherwise than through song and story.

The Commandment in question has been viewed by us mostly in its bearing upon the manufacture of idols. A second glace at it, however, discloses its full severity when laid upon a race of potential artists. Reread it with this thought in mind: "Thou shalt not make unto thee any graven image, nor any likeness of anything that is in heaven above, or that is in the earth beneath, or that is in the water under the earth." Let us not make the mistake of thinking that this law merely placed an embargo upon images to be used for idolatrous worship. The insurance guaranteed complete coverage against the damages of art, regardless of the motive inspiring it or the use to which it might be put. A thoroughly comprehensive explanation is provided in Deuteronomy, where we find a statement admitting of but one interpretation: "Take ye good heed unto yourselves lest ye make a graven image in the form of any figure, the likeness of male or female, the likeness of any beast that is upon the earth, the likeness of any winged bird that flieth in the heavens, the likeness of anything that creepeth on the ground, the likeness of any fish that is in the water under the earth . . . for Jehovah thy God is a devouring fire, a jealous God." Surely, after such an invoice of natural objects which dared not be imitated in art forms, there was little left for the Hebrew to draw, paint, or carve. His soul was destined to be forever locked up unless he found an outlet for it through his minstrelsy.

Naturally, he became a poet, a musician, a dramatist. All the pictures he dared not paint, all the statues he dared not carve, emerged through the word portraits which so beautifully adorn his chronicles, and the passionate fervor of songs unsurpassed for sheer strength and loveliness by the lyrical compositions of any people, either ancient or contemporaneous.

No artist should be held too vigorously to account for the minor inaccuracies he may commit in the interest of idealism. He is not out taking photographs, or making architectural blueprints. It is his right to distill his perceptions in the retort of his fancy. Persons who move upon such works with slide-rule and calipers are not equipped to deal generously enough with the artist type of self-expression. Sometimes one marvels at the gross dullness and bleak stupidity of such exegesis as attempts to parse words which had been used only because colors were not permissible, and diagram sentences intended only to be sung by antiphonal choirs. As reasonably might one make a tent of Venetian lace, or pave a street with Carrara marble.

Nor should any poet be brought to book for indulging his imagination. He has a right to assume that his product will be accepted on the same terms in which it was fabricated. If he says, "The curfew tolls the knell of parting day," he should be guaranteed that no tiresome exegete, three thousand years later, will write a solemn dissertation on the queer British belief that twilight was brought on by the ringing of a bell.

But if any poet, anywhere, is entitled to the full use of his imagination, how much more generosity should be shown to the Hebrew minstrel whose sole artistic vehicle was the epic. Around the history of his race he draped in graceful folds the mantle of legend. It is quite inconceivable that some one gifted composer fabricated a story adequate to explain and enshrine a notable event in the experience of the Israelites; a story thereafter to be repeated, by father to son, by priest to priest, without embellishment. Every telling of these

27

folk tales, about the evening camp fire, wrought its own magic on them. Anybody who thinks that seven hundred years of oral tradition could deliver, intact and unaltered, a volume of songs and stories to be engrossed upon the pages of history, should go back to school and learn something about the early composition of literature.

It is not to be considered a part of our present task even to speculate upon the nature of that urge which led Abraham out of Chaldea to found a new religion, much less to attempt the setting forth of the opinions offered by scholars especially concerned with this interesting migration. Whether and how the Absolute may have communicated with this image maker of Ur, counseling him to go out and found a separate nation uniquely questing the true God, and forsaking all the religious observances and beliefs identified with idolatry, is a problem quite beyond the scope of our study. Persons who wish to think that God revealed His will to Abraham, through a direct contact, have the ancient records for it, and are privileged to place their own interpretation upon it. Those who would account for the migration on another basis—some economic reason, perhaps—can have their guesses at the same price. When all are through guessing, the fact will remain that the Hebrews by some process arrived at a national and racial consciousness a very long time ago, centuries before that general era known to archæologists as the Bronze Age. For a nation to pledge itself to the worship of a God, spiritual and abstract, back in the Stone Age, and retain that motive for thirty-nine centuries, is worthy of note.

Their conception of Deity was so far in advance of their ideas about any and all other human interests that we will do well to consider this fact with care before resolving that Abraham left Chaldea for Canaan merely on a chance of finding better pasturage for the cattle.

Something, too, about the racial integrity of these queer people makes us pause and wonder. Their laws enjoined them against mixing with other races. No other law ever known among men has been more consistently and continuously obeyed, unless it be the law that what goes up must come down.

The Hebrew gathered all his facts around two foci —Jehovah and the Chosen People. Beginning with the conviction that Jehovah exerted Himself primarily, if not exclusively, in the interest of Israel, the minstrel saw His hand in all the affairs of the nation. If a city failed to befriend them, He wiped it out with fire and plague. If they fell into the toils of another nation, He opened a pathway through the sea, and they marched out dry-shod. If they were hungry, He rained down bread from heaven. If they were thirsty, He caused a stream of cold water to gush from a rock in the desert. The Old Testament brims with miracles.

Well-meant efforts have been made to offer adequate explanations from the field of the physical sciences for many of these alleged supernatural activities. The plagues of Egypt have been adroitly accounted for on the ground that an unusually deep inundation of the Nile Valley caused stagnant lagoons to breed noxious insects and reptiles, causing sickness among the cattle, and consequent physical disorders among the people. While it is not inconceivable that such a condition provided the structural foundation for the highly dramatic story of the plagues, it is idle to take the time and go to the bother of explaining this series of strange events on natural grounds, in face of the vast galaxy of Old Testament marvels for which no such treatment is available. When Elisha causes the axe to come to the surface of the river at a word of command, you either take the story or leave it.

Elijah the Tishbite puts the priests of Baal to rout on Mount Carmel, by calling down fire from heaven to consume a water-soaked altar of sacrifice. This has been nicely accounted for by a terrific electrical storm, the water furnishing the necessary conductor to invite the lightning's stroke. If this were the only wonder wrought in those days, the modern mind might waive aside the obvious objections to that theory, and accept the frail explanation offered. But all such fantastic endeavors to clear up the wonder world of the ancient Hebrews are futile when one considers the astounding number of miracles which resolutely refuse to be dealt with in this manner. However flexible the imagination may be in its ability to picture a strong east wind of sufficient velocity to open a dry path through the Red

Sea, there is no mind ingenious enough to account for Joshua's ability to make the sun stand still.

If anything of practical value—aside from the natural interest attaching to any ancient chronicle—is to be derived from these tales of wonders wrought by heavenly aid, it must accrue to us neither by an attempt to torture our credulity into a literal acceptance of these bizarre narratives nor a fatuous endeavor to explain them on natural grounds, but by listening for the overtones apparent in this Old World minstrelsy. We may be encouraged to this task by the sonorous words from that wise old book of Ecclesiasticus: "He that giveth his mind to the Most High, and is occupied in the meditation thereof, will seek out the wisdom of the ancients. . . . He will keep the sayings of men of renown. Where subtle parables are, there will he be also; and he will search for the hidden meaning of proverbs."

LINCOLN PUBLIC LIBRARY
LINCOLN, ILLINOIS

CHAPTER TWO

AN INEXHAUSTIBLE CRUSE

I

ALTHOUGH the chief center of inquiry, to anyone disturbed about the miracles, unquestionably
resides in the four gospels, we can afford to tarry in
the Old Testament long enough to examine a couple of
these delightful tales of Jehovah's magical intervention
in behalf of needy people. We will discover what practical value such stories may have for us today—lessons
taught by implication and inference.

At the moment, let us listen for the "overtones" in
the minstrelsy which sings of a miraculous cruse of oil
in the possession of a young widow who lived in the
days of Elisha, the bald-headed prophet.

By way of preparation for the practical study of
this event, it may be observed that the story invites
consideration of the doctrine of relativity as it applies
to ethical affairs.

All knowledge is relative. If I, with a scrappy,
desultory knowledge of a lot of things arrived at mostly
through the diligent use of open eyes, attentive ears,
and a greediness for books, should find myself in a
company of people who have gained all they know from
the tabloid newspapers and the movies, I am unques-

tionably a very wise man who should be listened to with respect. But should I happen to blunder in accidentally where a group of metaphysicians are sitting in conference, I would mentally shrivel until incapacitated to remain in that atmosphere any longer. I might easily leave the room unobserved; through the keyhole, perhaps.

Health is relative. If I, with a bad cold and three broken ribs, am seated in the waiting room of a cancer clinic, gazing about upon my companions who have real business there, I am well. There is nothing the matter with me at all. I would be a mere hypochondriac if I complained of an ache or discomfort. If, however, I am at home with said cold and broken ribs, associating with a family that is entirely normal, I am a sick man, entitled to all the rights and privileges thereto pertaining.

Physical strength is relative. I can give almost anybody quite a vigorous tussle in the Home for the Aged. My services would not be required should the varsity team need a full-back in the fourth quarter.

Wealth is relative. I have been in companies where I felt quite well blessed with what the world had doled out to me in the form of material benefits. I have been in places where I required only a tin cup and a handful of lead pencils to give my mendicancy suitable credentials.

I must keep these matters in mind as I study the story of the miraculous oil cruse.

II

It was in the days of the great Elisha who served as dean of the prophets during a period when the king of Israel was a half wit and the queen was an assassin. Elisha had gathered about him a group of young men, and had established a theological seminary for the training of prophets.

Word had just arrived that one of the alumni of Elisha's school was dead. The tidings were brought by the young widow, herself. She also reported, tearfully, that her late husband's estate consisted only of two boys and a miscellaneous assortment of floating bills—not an unusual legacy for a prophet to devise and bequeath to his widow.

Moreover, the two boys were to be attached by the creditors, to work until the debts were discharged out of their wages. What could she do to avert this tragedy?

Elisha, being a very practical person, inquired about her assets. "What have you?" he queried.

"Nothing!" she replied.

"You mean that literally?"

"Exactly! There is nothing in my house, at this moment, but a cruse of oil!" And that was, relatively speaking, and as compared with the extent of her indebtedness, nothing.

Elisha spent a studious moment. The easy and obvious way out of the difficulty was to give this woman a note of introduction to a few of the more substantial and philanthropic people in her late husband's diocese, a letter running somewhat as follows:

"To Whom This May Concern:

The bearer is the widow of a young prophet recently graduated from our school. He was a good man, as many of you know, and his early death is greatly to be regretted.

His sudden departure made it impossible for him to put his affairs in order, and there are some debts which seem to be immediately pressing. Indeed, the two little boys are to be bound out in manual service as surety for the payment of these obligations, unless prompt steps are taken to liquidate.

This good woman is quite destitute. I have it on her testimony that there is nothing in her house but a cruse of oil.

This note is to inquire whether, in your opinion, the case is not deserving of substantial sympathy; and, if so, will you not contribute something toward this worthy woman's relief?

I suggest that you might give her a pot of oil. If all the benevolently disposed persons in your locality will donate, each, one pot of oil, the unfortunate situation may be cleared."

"It really wouldn't, though," reflected Elisha, as he finished the imaginary composition of the letter. "It would be only temporary and inadequate relief. She would be back here again by Tuesday, wondering what to do next. One mustn't pauperize the woman. She is too fine to be a beggar. I'll think again."

Presently he said: "You go home and visit every house in your neighborhood. Ask every family for the loan of an oil pot. An empty one. They will have plenty of oil jugs, oil jars, and oil pots to spare; and when you ask for the loan of an empty one they will be so glad you did not ask for the donation of a full one that they will give you the very largest vessel on the premises. Carry these pots home. Set them in a row outside your house. Take one of these empty oil pots into your own room. Shut the door. Shut it tightly. Let no one in; not even your children. And then, alone, you are to pour out oil from your cruse into the empty oil pot until it is filled.

"No, no!" Elisha silenced the objection he saw in the woman's face, and the protest budding on her lips. "No, no! You do as I say! No matter how big the borrowed oil pot may be, your cruse will be ample to fill it. And you are to continue to pour from your cruse until you have filled this borrowed vessel. Then put it outside and take another. Do not be discouraged if it seems to come slowly at first. Just keep on pouring; and when you have filled all the borrowed vessels, sell the oil, pay your debts, and live without fear."

Mystified, but obedient—for surely the celebrated prophet's word should be believed—the widow went home; made sure that her one little cruse of oil was safe; started out on her campaign to borrow empty oil pots.

The first place she visited—if we may be privileged to lend this tale a helping hand in the way of minor incident, for all we have of it in the text is the bare bones—the first place she visited was the home of the Ben Ezra family who lived in a big house at the top of the hill. The Ben Ezras were quite well-to-do as people went in that vicinity. Old Ben Ezra himself sat out on the front veranda in a wheeled chair with a shawl about his narrow shoulders, the fringes falling over his twisted and helpless hands.

"An empty oil pot?" echoed old Ben Ezra in a squeaking treble. "To be sure, my dear; as many as you like!"

"Just one," said the widow, with a smile. She entered the house, and a servant found her an oil pot. While she waited she had a word of greeting for old Rachel Ben Ezra, who, through an open doorway, was to be seen propped up with pillows in bed, endeavoring to knit with the four fingers her rheumatism had not yet put entirely out of commission.

The oil pot in her arms, the young widow set off for

home, with mind busy. It was a huge oil pot, this one of the crippled Ben Ezras', but as she marched along, scarcely noticing its weight upon her supple strength, she already felt almost confident that she could fill it from her own cruse and possibly have some oil left over.

She put down the Ben Ezra oil pot at her own door and struck off in another direction, this time across the fields to the Asher family. The Ashers, man and wife, lived in a very trim, prim, tidy house, where everything was always quiet—a striking contrast to her own, in which toys littered the floor and youthful voices occasionally made the welkin ring. The Asher house was quiet—almost too quiet. Nobody had ever marred the furniture, soiled the paint, broken a window with a ball, nor left little muddy footmarks on the rugs in the Asher house; for they were childless.

The widow tapped softly at the door and was admitted. She made her request and was cheerfully accommodated. She took up the Ashers' empty oil jar under her arm, and all the way across the fields *en route* from that silent house she could hear the echoes of her little boys' laughter as they played in their tiny garden; and she knew, almost certainly, that she would be able to pour this empty jar full and maybe have some oil remaining in her cruse.

Having deposited the Ashers' empty vessel beside the one she had borrowed from the Ben Ezras', the widow went across the road to see if perhaps Widow Mattanah might lend her one. Widow Mattanah had been left very well provided for, and surely she would oblige her neighbor. Unfortunately, she was blind. "Oh yes, gladly enough" would she lend an empty oil jar—a big one. Yes, she knew where they were. She could find it easily.

Together they went down into the gloom of the cellar. "I wonder how you find your way about, down here," said the younger woman. "It's very dark!"

"Yes, it's very dark," replied Widow Mattanah in a tone of unmistakable resentment and rebellion. "It's very dark everywhere—down here, and up on the terrace. The sky is dark, too. There is no sun in it by day, and no stars by night. Here, my child, is the largest one I have. Can you lift it?"

She could. Not only could she lift it, but she could fill it, when the time came for the great experiment. Her heart was pounding with the excitement of hope.

On the way to her house she passed the weak-minded boy of the Ammiel family, stumbling along through the dust with the beastlike half trot of imbecility, his wan face distorted and his claw fingers fumbling at his soiled scarf; and she decided she would go over to the Ammiels' and see if perhaps they might lend her an empty oil jar. She felt very certain that the Ammiel family had one, and she knew that she could fill it to the brim.

So all that day she went about collecting empty oil pots, which she placed in a row outside her little house.

The very first one she carried into her room, when all ready for the great adventure, was the last one she had borrowed, over at the Kohaths', where she had found a family brawl in full blast—Father Kohath, with two boys and one girl, aligned in warm and gusty battle against Mother Kohath and two girls and one boy.

As she had entered, Father Kohath was in the act of disinheriting his son Aaron, and Mother Kohath was replying, with considerable vigor, that if Aaron went she was going, too; and Father Kohath retorted that such measures would be satisfactory provided she took with her Rebecca and Hannah.

At this juncture the widow had inquired if she could borrow an empty oil pot; and as they were all too busy with their exciting engagement to leave the scene of battle at that moment, they told her to go out to the spring house and help herself. Mother Kohath added, as she turned away. "Take them all! We're breaking up housekeeping, anyway!"

The widow wanted only one of the Kohath oil jars, however, the one jar that would be emblematic of all the Kohath jars (if one may be forgiven this slight digression from the main thesis).

For three hundred yards, she could hear the Kohaths still exchanging the usual amenities after the Kohathian manner, and she felt sure she could fill their oil pot in the tranquillity of her little home, where no petulant word had ever been spoken. So she tried that one first.

She did not invite anyone in to see the experiment. Almost certainly the friendly neighbor whose counsel she might have sought would say: "What? Fill that big jar of Kohaths'—out of that little cruse? Nonsense! You're sick. You've been worrying too much. Sit down, now, and let me make you a cup of tea."

No. Elisha was right. Here was a situation in which nobody could be of any help at all. Not even her own family. She would have to see this pouring act through alone. So out of her little she began to pour. Here was the Kohaths' oil jar. She stood before it meditatively. Yes, she was poor; but she wasn't that poor! Never in her life had she been so utterly luckless as these wretched people who wallowed daily in a welter of mutual misunderstanding and bitterness. Compared with the emptiness of that which symbolized the Kohath misfortune, she was rich; her life was full. Her little cruse that her husband had given her took on a peculiar magic, and she poured the huge Kohath vessel brimming! And set it aside and took up another—the borrowed oil jar of the young wife of Namal, Namal who had absconded with three golden talents belonging to his employer and hadn't been heard of for six moons. Out of her memory of her departed husband's love and loyalty the young widow of the prophet poured the precious libation of an undishonored

41

recollection into the drear emptiness of the Namal vessel, and was rich, rich, rich!

III

Which things, as Paul would say, are an allegory. Whoever wants to believe that the widow of the prophet, upon the advice of Elisha, poured oil from a magic cruse until she had filled all her neighbors' jars to the brim, thus creating enough wealth to free her of her financial entanglements, has the story for it, and can give it whatever credence it seems to deserve. But those who accept this ancient legend on the basis of allegory probably get as much from the tale as the literalist, and something more.

By this allegorical interpretation, we need not try to content ourselves with a story of Old World legerdemain, by which one unfortunate woman was miraculously relieved of her distress through the supernatural act of a magic cruse (a story very like many another in the folk lore and fables of all peoples the world over) but steps the story up into the realm of reality for every needy soul who, from the slender cruse of acknowledged blessings, pours riches of the type which moth and rust cannot corrupt, or thieves break through and steal.

Searching for that which stimulates, enriches, and enlarges life, the restless roam about in quest of healing springs, acres of diamonds, fairer scenes, firmer friends.

They are not aware that from the magic cruse in their own possession they might pour out all the benefits they have the talent to enjoy.

It is not inconceivable that the skilled exegetical expert, having read this interpretation of the miracle of the widow's cruse, will chuckle, and remark, "Claptrap!"

Were we to study this story with the same microscope and tweezers that his research enjoins upon him, we, too, would be forced to decide that our process of analysis hasn't a leg to stand on, and deserves no respect.

But we were only listening for the "overtones" in this ancient minstrel's lay, and one doesn't hunt for overtones with microscope and tweezers.

CHAPTER THREE

A CHEST OF RELICS

I

HOW the introduction of a beauteous ideal into ugly surroundings can transform an otherwise irremediable situation to such extent that it is easier to account for the change on the basis of a miracle than to explain it on physical grounds, is implied in the tale of a wonder-working chest of relics during its brief residence in the home of one Obed-edom the Gittite, early in the reign of King David.

It is no part of our present inquiry to figure on how much of fact and how much of legend combine to furnish the intriguing tales of miracles effected by the Ark of the Covenant in the days of Israel's endeavor to repossess the promised land.

We are rather to concern ourselves with a single episode which has not received the attention it richly deserves, probably for the reason that it is driven into almost total eclipse by other more dramatic narratives contingent to this story of the miracle wrought upon the Obed-edom household.

Assuming the reader's knowledge of the most stirring stanzas of that epic which relates to the Ark of the Covenant, its prominent place in early Hebrew worship, its unique talismanic virtues in times of battle, its reputed capacity to clear the way of obstacles for the pilgrim host, we may proceed to a sketchy survey of conditions at the beginning of David's reign when the nation was in despair and nobody knew quite what ailed the chosen people except that lately they had been in sore straits.

David suspected that Jehovah was displeased over some failure on the part of the nation to comply with the ordinances which guaranteed prosperity. In quest of such delinquencies, the king learned that the Ark of the Covenant had long since disappeared from its place of reverence at the capital, and upon inquiry discovered, to his surprise and chagrin, that this magic chest was lost.

Hastily organizing scouting parties to search for the venerated ark, David gave himself diligently to pursuing every lead that gave promise of disclosing the hiding place of this ancient treasure. He was at length rewarded by the news that the chest was stored in a little town at the southern tip of his kingdom.

By nature fond of pageantry, David easily resolved to bring the Ark of the Covenant back to his capital in a manner that would atone for the long neglect of this hallowed emblem of Jehovah's providence. He called out the musicians and the army. On an appointed day the garish procession moved across country, *en route* to "the little city of the woods," to secure the

45

golden chest and return it in state to its erstwhile seat of honor.

Apparently everybody had forgotten—priests and all —that this potential thing was to be carried by certain picked men from a specified tribe who were to bear it by the staves fastened to either side of the chest. David, ignorant of this regulation, ordered the ark to be placed upon a new cart and hauled by oxen at the head of the procession. The fact that it was a new cart did not make the infraction of the old law for the proper transportation of the ark any less serious. David may have had plans for placing that cart in the national museum after its errand had been performed. But the cart technique was all wrong, as the king was presently to discover.

With great rejoicing, triumphant chants, and impressive ceremonies the stately pilgrimage set forth on the homeward march. All was going according to David's hopes until the oxen stumbled over some obstruction in the road. A guard marching by the side of the vehicle put out his hand in a well-intended effort to steady the ark and instantly fell dead at the touch of this dynamic thing; the procession halted abruptly; the band ceased playing in the middle of a measure; the choir quit on a diminished seventh; the pilgrimage was in complete consternation.

A conference was held. Inquiry revealed the depressing fact that there was not a priest present who remembered how the Ark of the Covenant should be borne to insure safety to those who carried it. A decision was reached to leave the golden chest in the first house they came to, and make no further efforts to return it to the capital until the ancient records had been investigated for the laws pertaining to its safe conduct. The nearest house was the home of Obed-edom the Gittite.

II

At this point our imagination takes us by the sleeve and leads us up the road to inspect the home of the Obed-edom family. It was a squalid, shabby, unkempt little house, and the Obed-edoms fitted nicely into their environment.

This was going to be a great day for the Obed-edoms, they thought; for the news had come that the gorgeous procession was to pass along their highway and they would have a chance to see it all from their own doorstep. Not very often did anything interesting happen to the Obed-edom family, for they were poor and off the beat of exciting events. This morning they were up early, gazing eagerly toward the southeast, the little ones toeing the lower rail of the picket fence, and the older children perched on the roof of the decayed granary. Presently one of the boys gave a shout that brought the whole family to attention, Father and Mother Obed-edom hurrying out to join the excited children in the front yard.

Young Samuel had seen a golden glint of sunshine flash its reflection from a polished shield. Now the distant cavalcade began to take shape. It was really coming! The little girls hugged each other with delight. In a half hour, the glittering pageant was in full detail. What a riot of color! How splendid!

When but a few hundred yards away, the procession abruptly halted. Even the bucolic Obed-edoms sensed an accident. Something very dreadful had happened. One could tell by the way the music stopped and the apparent excitement of the people in the vanguard. None of the Obed-edoms spoke, but each knew there was some manner of tragedy connected with this sudden halt.

They saw a group of gray-faced priests gingerly lift a great golden box from the cart, the choir scattering to give them plenty of room. And now it was coming up the road toward their house. Father Obed-edom swallowed convulsively when he noticed that the priests were looking his way. They stopped at the gate, turned in, halted, and their spokesman announced that they were afraid to carry the ark any farther. It had just killed a man who had accidentally touched it—a good man, too, who was trying only to steady it on the jostling cart. They would have to go back, he said, to the capital, and find out how this magical chest was to be treated; for no one could tell what it might do next. Meantime, by order of the king, the golden chest was to be left here, in this house, for safe keeping. The

Obed-edoms shuddered and grew pale. In their house? How dreadful!

Father Obed-edom made no outcry. It was not customary to debate the king's command. The kind of democracy that argues with its betters had not yet become popular. So the Obed-edoms stood, open-eyed and open-mouthed, watching the golden chest go through their front doorway. They noted with what becoming reverence the priests handled it and what pains they took to avoid any ill-timed familiarities with it. Then the bearers came out of the house, drawing long breaths indicative of satisfaction that a solemn duty had been performed with due regard for the honor of their national talisman; the procession was reorganized quietly; a word of command was given; the pilgrimage was in motion. Silently it padded past the little house of the Obed-edoms, slowly disappeared over the shoulder of the hill, and the stunned family was alone with the *Thing!*

No, it does not say in Chronicles that the Obed-edoms were frightened completely out of their wits, but one has a right to deduce as much from the story. If a huge crowd of many thousands were to stop in front of your house and announce that they were going to deposit in your living room a box that they considered entirely too dangerous to handle, you would not be very much obliged for the honor. You would watch the disappearance of these people with great anxiety; and when they were all gone and you were

49

left alone with this capricious explosive, you would be scared. There is no question that that is the way the Obed-edoms felt about it.

All that afternoon they wandered about the premises, speaking in whispers; and that evening they sat, in the deepening dusk, on the kitchen steps, huddled together in an agony of fear. That night they slept in the barn on the straw.

Early next morning Father Obed-edom, Samuel, and Jepthah remembered some important work that had to be done in the far corner of the farm, and left early. It was suspected that they wished to put as much distance as possible between themselves and the terrible guest. Mother Obed-edom and the girls reluctantly entered the kitchen and went about their usual tasks.

Feminine curiosity was probably well armed with valor, even in the long ago. Without doubt, Mother Obed-edom found herself at the open door of the living room before the morning was very far advanced. What a gorgeously beautiful thing it was—this Ark of the Covenant. She stood in rapt contemplation of the glory of it; the exquisite carvings; the gold embossments. A wave of chagrin swept over her as she took stock of that untidy, squalid room. What a mean place to offer as the sanctuary of this holy thing. She called to her elder daughters, and they came. It was quite unnecessary to explain to them how wide was the difference between the beauty of this silent guest and the poor hospitality their home afforded. The girls went out into the woods and fields, returning in an hour, their arms loaded with ferns and flowers and leafy branches. Mother Obed-edom was found by them, when they came in, deftly sketching the main motif for the rug she proposed to weave, carrying in the corners the symbols of worshiping angels.

Somewhat after noon, Father Obed-edom and the boys came home. Fear is an important sentiment, but hunger can put up quite a doughty struggle with it; so the male contingent had finished the work in the far pasture and were now ready to be fed. They were invited in to see what changes had occurred in the distinguished room.

"I might have known you would take some foolish chances," grumbled Obed-edom. "Thought I told you to stay away from there."

Nevertheless, he followed them to the door and looked in, breathing hard and saying nothing. When he returned to the kitchen, he remarked that there were some long cobwebs on the ceiling over the golden chest, which looked very badly. Mother Obed-edom replied that she was not tall enough to get them down and had hoped he might do so. It pleased Obed-edom to be thought so capable. Thus have wives secured the services of their husbands for a great many millennia. Obed-edom rose to the challenge and fetched down the cobwebs. He also decided that the walls and ceiling of the wretched living room needed redecoration.

That afternoon he and the boys began to paint. When they were through with the living room and his damaged self-respect was returning as he glowed with pride over this task performed in honor of the beautiful Ark of the Covenant, Obed-edom noticed how grimy and shabby the other rooms had suddenly become, by comparison. The painting enterprise went on. The whole interior of the house was beautified. Then they painted the outside of the house and mended the chimney. They painted the fence, which was then so conspicuously ugly that they tore it down and planted shrubbery. Samuel and Jepthah clipped the lawn and laid out flower beds in artistic patterns, under the supervision of their sisters. Beauty had magically become epidemic.

None of them could tolerate the shabby appearance of the barn, the granary, the spring house, and the implement sheds, now that their home had taken on such fine new aspirations. The painting business continued. The plough was mended; the harrow was supplied with a full complement of teeth; the axe got a better handle; the chisels took on a keener edge. Work came easier, now that the tools were more effective. It did not take long to make two more looms for the girls. They seemed anxious to have better clothes to suit the changing environment.

Now the thrilling quest of beauty began to affect the inner character of the Obed-edoms. Where, hitherto, their voices had been shrill and petulant at breakfast, it was easy to detect a general mellowness of tone in the presence of this contagious ideal. The Obed-edoms took on a new culture. Their entire attitude toward one another was transformed. They began to prosper materially. And it was not long until the neighbors were spreading the report that a miracle had been wrought in the house of Obed-edom because the Ark of the Covenant was there. It was true. The Ark had performed a miracle—exactly such a miracle as may be effected in any home or any heart where a beautiful ideal enters, driving out all the ugliness and meanness just by the fact of its presence.

David comes back in three months, with another parade and sound information about the proper handling of the Ark. It is carried out through the Obed-edoms' front door and reverentially borne to the capital.

Query: Did the Obed-edoms slip back to the old degradation, the old quarrels, the old cobwebs? I like to think that the memory of that hallowed thing, whose presence had graced their poor home, was enough to motivate them in a continued search for added beauty of soul and environment.

Now, anybody who wants to take his Chronicles straight is fully entitled to believe that in some mysterious manner Jehovah "blessed the house of Obed-edom, and all that he had." I, too, believe this. But I find it so much more plausible to think that the miracle was performed in terms which might, in God's good providence, occur again. It seems to me it would

be ever so much more delightful a miracle if, instead
of being restricted to the enrichment of the Obed-
edoms, it might happen almost any time, to almost
anybody, almost anywhere.

Of course, the transformation wrought in the primitive home of the Obed-edoms could proceed only a
very little way toward what we now know as beauty.
Given the same type of idealism today, we can go
much farther with it. Our ideals can perform greater
works; but, in essence, they operate by the everlasting
technique. It's the Obed-edom miracle, after all.
There is something very commanding about beauty.
When it once gets going in a house it has its way—provided the inhabitants do not conspire to destroy it.

CHAPTER FOUR

UNWROUGHT MIRACLES

I

WHOEVER enters upon a serious study of Jesus' reputed miracles with intent to learn something about the nature of the divine energy accessible to the Master will find it of advantage to spend considerable time and thought, at the outset, on the stories of his stout refusal, on certain occasions, to employ any other power than the natural fortitude of the normal soul.

If we can discover what problems of life are to be solved—when and if they are solved—without the solicitation of any more strength than has been naturally bequeathed to us, we may be well on our way toward an understanding of the practical uses to which divine power may be put in our own experience.

It is safe to say that any investigation of the miraculous element in Jesus' career may properly begin at the point of his temptation in the wilderness to turn stones into bread.

Familiar as this story is to the conscientious student of Christianity, one suspects that its stupendous significance has been but feebly expressed and inadequately appreciated. This event in the Master's experience is of such vast importance in its bearing upon his entire

55

life program and the essentials of his teachings, that not to understand it in all its manifold implications is to have missed the very structural thesis of his gospel. Without a full comprehension of what was at issue, in the wilderness, most of the parables fail to yield up their richest treasures, and the Sermon on the Mount is as a chest of precious jewels for which the finder has no key.

Some thoughtful and well-informed reader may suggest that other indications of the miraculous element in Jesus' life are recorded of him prior to this event in the Jeshimon Wilderness. We should pause to inquire if this be true.

It may be taken by common consent that the miracle stories pertaining to Jesus' birth do not properly fall within the scope of our study. Whatever importance is to be attached to them, they are not, strictly speaking, miracles of Jesus.

But, lest some one may think we are disposed to dodge the issue, because of reluctance to offer an opinion on a matter so full of controversial queries, let us give the nativity stories a hasty glance, and then be on to our more important investigation of the miracles predicated of the Master.

It is no more necessary to a proper appraisal of Jesus' ministry of love and sacrifice that we should know he was born in a manger at Bethlehem of Judæa, than it is necessary to a proper appraisal of Napoleon's career of selfishness and slaughter that we should know he was born on a doorstep in the Isle of Corsica.

Indeed, there are many thoughtful people who feel that enough misunderstanding has arisen, in respect to Jesus, by way of a too slavish interpretation of these nativity legends, to make them more honored by the breach than the observance. But, fully realizing the difficulties involved, it may be believed that the world would have been the loser had we not received these stories at the hands of those pious mystics who sincerely wished their spiritual posterity to have the highest possible esteem and veneration for their Lord, and knew no better way of accounting for the majesty of his character than to record of him all the supernatural incidents which the minstrels recited concerning his infancy.

Now that we are so remote from the time and place of the origin of these stories, about the only essential questions that may be raised concerning them are: Do they mean anything in present life? Do they add anything to our proper appreciation of Jesus? Does it make him more potential, in our regard, to believe them true?

If one assumes these narratives to be legendary, has one demolished the story of Jesus and consigned him to the category of mythical heroes? Not at all. A legend may be unhistorical, and still contain more impressionistic history, and afford a more faithful portrait of facts, than the statistical records, sworn and subscribed to by cold-blooded annalists.

Colonial history, as embalmed by the official scribes of the period, knows nothing whatsoever about one Paul Revere who rode out the Lexington pike, warning the farmers against the invasion of their predatory cousins from England. But when Longfellow caught up this insignificant item about Paul Revere and his midnight ride and tinted the episode with enough colors to make it captivating to the imagination, he handed American youth an idealistic portrait of the revolution, its cause, its spirit, its valor, its suffering, its poverty, and its patriotism, which all the exact chronicles ever written of that epoch had failed to disclose.

Actual history gives the names of the commanding officers, the dates of the military movements, the number of troops employed, the strategies enacted, and the results achieved; but history cannot make real the spirit of the cause at issue, or the sentiment of the people participant in it. You have to look to the minstrel for all that. He knows how to draw a circle around some little incident that the professional scribe would never pause to look at; and within that illumined circle you are invited to behold the human interests at work. You see the whole thing in miniature. When Paul Revere mounts his horse and the lights flash out from the old church tower, you have a faithful picture of the Colonial cause.

All important literature is built on this hypothesis;

and were it not for the poets' stories of apparently trifling episodes in the past, we would be as devoid of actual knowledge concerning certain major events, in the ages past, as if no history had been written of them at all.

The two pedigrees of Jesus, presented in Matthew and Luke, need not worry us. They disagree too seriously for both of them to be accepted as of historical value. One of them traces Jesus' genealogy from Abraham to Joseph, and the other from Adam to Joseph, in connection with explaining how Joseph was not related to Jesus at all; so one learns nothing from these genealogical tables except a very definite impression of the naïveté of the minstrels to whom a logically consistent story was apparently of much less concern than the presentation of an idealistic portrait of their hero. To learn this much, however, from these conflicting pedigrees, is to have started the chronicle in the proper state of mind.

The great King Herod, who in actual fact was a petty consular officer in the employ of the Roman government at an hour when Augustus Cæsar had enough important foreign problems on his hands without inviting unnecessary complications with the Jews, is presented as a type of imperial power resentful of any movement looking toward the people's liberty. Jesus had come to set the captives free and make every man conscious of his divine sonship. The world must have this portrait of the Master as a liberator. Naturally the imperial interests of the world would resent the advent of such an emancipator and make an effort to thwart his purpose. The minstrel, knowing no better way of setting forth this condition than by the pictorial method customary with his guild, makes Herod the symbol of earthly political power. And having determined to paint his picture in colors sufficiently vivid to outlast the years, the poet has Herod butcher all the little babies in the vicinity of Bethlehem, so ardent is his resolve to see that the infant Jesus does not live to accomplish this promised liberation of the common people from their bondage.

Of course the difficulties involved in the story, if one attempts to view it as of historical value, rather than of impressionistic value, are quite insurmountable. While King Herod's sleuths scour the country and beat the bushes to find the potential babe, Jesus' parents publicly present him at the temple for the customary ceremonials, where songs are sung frankly avowing him to be the predicted king. But, unable to find the child, Herod's men stage a campaign of slaughter on all classes of boy babies in that part of the province. While this holocaust of horror is on, Joseph and Mary journey to Egypt to find sanctuary for the wondrous child, returning only after the danger is over and Herod dead. Matthew adds that the trip was made "that it might be fulfilled which was spoken of the Lord by the prophet, saying, 'Out of Egypt have I called my son.'"

Now, if, after all this, anybody feels that the slaughter of the innocents is to be accepted as historically correct, we can only say that his credulity is surely as remarkable as the story itself.

We are only expected to see here a group of types symbolizing important forces at work in the story of Jesus. Herod is a type. He stands for the political empire that dares not let a liberating tendency loose in society. We must permit the minstrel to sing his song, without weighing it on the scales.

Wise men from the East, led by a star, come with gifts for the new king. They are types, and their gifts are symbolic. For ages, the world's seers had been toiling on the problem of humanity's relation to the heights. The best they had deduced concerning kingliness was that gold was imperative to its success: they brought him gold. The best they had deduced about man's proper method of seeking God's favor was through worship, involving prayer and sacrifice: they brought him incense. The best they had deduced about man's ultimate state was the importance of a reverential attitude toward his corpse: they brought him myrrh. This is a very beautiful story; rich in symbolism; magnificently conceived. But it must read with understanding or its meaning is decidedly cloudy.

Not for a very great deal would we part with the poem of the Star of Bethlehem. We do not have to study astronomy to find out which of the planets gracing the sky has shed the brightest light and conferred the highest benefits upon mankind. Of all the stars in the heavens, that star is the most luminous. If it never rose, except in the pious imagination of a minstrel in whose regard Jesus deserved an announcement from the firmament, that in no way dims its light for the understanding heart.

The angels sing to the shepherds of good will as the price of peace among men. World experience has proved that the angels were correct; the song true. The minstrel was right in believing that if the angels sang of good will as the condition upon which peace would come, they sang it to the shepherds. If peace is to come through good will, the shepherds will have to believe and practice it first of all people. No use singing it to diplomats assembled around council tables in peace parliaments. The movement must start out in the country. Ah, these minstrels knew a thing or two about the subject they are discussing. They do not compose their songs on the spot. Luke is not standing by, that night, with notebook in hand, jotting down memoranda. The epic which involves the song of the angels is composed long after it had been made clear what Jesus taught about the imperatives of world salvation. Peace would come through good will. Jesus taught it. It was true. Luke lets the angels sing it to the shepherds. A transcendently beautiful story, when properly viewed. Of all the sublime oratorios ever sung, which is the greatest? The song of the angels. Do you believe it ever happened in actual

fact? No. Is it important that you should? No.
Do you still believe that the song of the angels to the
shepherds was the greatest song ever sung? Yes.
That's fine. Now we're really getting somewhere with
this business. If you have arrived at that point of
spiritual discernment where you take no stock in the
historical merits of the angelic choir, but are firmly
convinced that this chorus of angels sang to the shepherds the most important message ever conveyed on the
wings of harmony, you are ready to go on to a serious
study of Jesus' strange career.

II

Perhaps a miracle is implied in the report of the child
Jesus' conference with the rabbis in the temple where
he is said to have astonished these learned men with
the cogency of his queries and the lucidity of his comments; but since we are not informed what matters
were under discussion, nor exactly what Jesus said,
we lack the data which might enable us to risk an
opinion whether the lad was speaking supernaturally or
with the precocity of an unusually gifted boy of twelve.
The student will be well within his rights if he refuses
to consider this temple event as a disclosure of supernormal power, even assuming that he accepts the narrative at face value, which he may not care to do.

We must delete all the tales of wonders wrought
by the boy Jesus on the streets of Nazareth, as reported

in certain apocryphal writings, on the ground of their obvious inconsistency. The omission of such a document as "The First Gospel of the Infancy" from the New Testament canon was not determined upon because it had no standing in the esteem of the early church fathers, for the "gospel" in question was fully accepted in the second century by so influential a sect as the Gnostics, and furnished citations appearing with frequency in the works of such eminent Christian leaders as Eusebius and Chrysostum. No; these alleged "gospels" which failed to gain admission into the canonical scriptures were discredited only because they reported of the Master certain bizarre, capricious, and occasionally cruel and unwarranted exhibitions of magical power which intruded a dissonant note into the symphony of love, compassion, and humility produced by his appeals to the finest impulses of the human heart.

Any early document which predicated of Jesus spectacular feats clearly out of harmony with the ideals upon which his saviourhood rests was repudiated as spurious, regardless of the esteem in which it might have been held by primitive mystics. Stories of the boy Jesus' manufacture of clay pigeons which flew away, and other tales of the sort which not only bear all the marks of untrustworthiness but teach nothing worth their preservation, may be waived aside.

And by the same logic, we may very properly minify the importance of any narrative, even in the canonical gospels, which either by implication disputes or

by indirection fails to confirm the essential ethics of
the Galilean culture. It may or may not be important to try to believe that Jesus blasted a fruitless fig
tree with a word of condemnation. Persons who see
in that reported act of Jesus any indication of a petu-
lance that could not endure a slight disappointment
without invoking divine power to wreak vengeance on a
barren tree, will vastly improve their estimate of the
Master by refusing to credit the story as it stands. If
their imagination is good for an interpretation of this
event which makes it symbolic of some important spiritual fact, let them make such use of the narrative. If
they find nothing helpful here, let them decide they
do not know what it is about, and pass on.

Whatever may be the technique of our thoughtful
discrimination between the records which picture an
idealistic, kindly, brotherly, sympathetic Christ, and the
occasional stories which fail to present him at full
stature, we must positively insist upon a clear, har-
monious, consistent portrait of one who went about
doing good, who came to heal, to bind up the broken-
hearted; a portrait of divine love in action; a selfless,
magnanimous soul, quite beyond the reach of the petty
vexations and puerile impetuosities which we find so
unlovely in ourselves and would eradicate by an earnest
striving to be more like Jesus.

Whatever reported episodes in the gospels, or anywhere else, cloud or impair that vision must be ap-
praised very much as our wise church fathers dealt with

the documents now known as apocryphal. However important it may be that we avoid any ruthless mutilation of the Scriptures, it is considerably more important that we permit no mutilation of the spiritual portrait of Christ, who humbled himself and became as a servant, that through his poverty we might be rich. Anything that does not ring true to that primary hypothesis must be omitted from consideration. His kingdom was not of this world; his majesty was not of the type wherein doth sit the awe of kings; his displays of supernormal power were not the feats of a magician, eager to bewilder the senses and thus enhance his repute as a person of extraordinary endowments. He was bent on rendering constructive service of the sort which any unselfish, faith-filled altruist might render the social order, by consistently following his program of vital contact with God and complete self-abnegation. Whatever pigments have been used on the traditional picture of Christ, which fail to blend harmoniously into the enduring colors instinctively accepted by Christian civilization as indubitably authentic, are fading. Perhaps modern criticism has been too impatient to dispose of such tones in the conventional portrait, and, in attempting to efface them with the sharp acids of academic inquiry, may be in danger of injuring the fabric. It may be believed that the safest test of these hues is Time. Gamaliel's decision, in this respect, was right.

III

The student of Jesus' miracles can well afford to spend as much time as he can possibly spare to the full story of the events which transpired in the Jeshimon Wilderness. Had the Christian order paid one-tenth the attention to the significance of all that occurred in the Jeshimon that it has devoted to strange doings in and about Bethlehem, we would have a better-informed Christianity and possibly a more enlightened world.

Here is a story curiously kaleidoscopic in structure. Put the glass to your eye, and you will see first the Jeshimon Wilderness as a barren, fearsome, lonesome district bounded on the east by the Dead Sea and irregularly merging into settled and more or less fertile country slightly east of the general longitude of Jericho. Torrential rains beat it hard for a few days, annually, converting its arroyos into rivers which magically vanish as the sun blisters and glazes the arid rocks and sand into the semblance of a topographical relief, done in alum. A few half-starved rodents scurry about through the parched wadies. Noxious insects abound. Snakes glide through the crevices of the rocks. Lizards sprawl, panting, on the hot crags. It is a cheerless, leafless, forsaken country. The first view is not promising to the student, informed that here is the stage where the most strategic act of Jesus' ministry is to occur.

Shift the glass ever so slightly, and you become

aware of a well-worn, active caravan trail laterally bisecting this region; and, on that trail heavily freighted pack camels may be seen rhythmically trudging westward, *en route* to the Mediterranean, loaded to capacity with salt from the flats which rim the saltest of all salt seas. Now, this view of the Jeshimon is tremendously important, for it explains the Roman interest in Judæa at the hour with which we are concerned. Salt was one of the world's most rare and valuable staples. It was so precious and difficult to obtain that Rome had even paid her soldiers their dole in discs of salt; and but for the necessity of Rome to traverse that old salt trail, and the Jews' objection to Rome's having a right of way through Judæa, it is exceedingly doubtful if Augustus would have gone to the bother and expense of maintaining consular offices and garrisons in that remote locality, now entirely off the highway of active commerce and diversified industry—an impoverished, sullen, unproductive, discouraged land and people, with slender natural resources and but little talent for fabricating art treasures or marketable wares.

The most promising place in Judæa, therefore, to find whatever was alive and in direct contact with the outside world was on that busy old salt trail through the Jeshimon. And while the first sight of it is bleak and drear, one comes to understand that if anybody desired to make an announcement of concern to the working world of active affairs, his most strategic rostrum was not to be found on the temple plaza in Jerusalem, but in the lonely defiles of the wilderness.

With this information in mind, another slight shift of the glass discloses a bronzed ascetic, wandering up and down the parched ravines of that Judæan desert, feeding on locusts and wild honey, hailing passing caravans to tell his strange story of a coming king who was destined to raise up an empire far greater than any earthly dominion—a king who would appear with divine credentials to wreak heavenly vengeance upon a wicked and perverse generation.

Another turn of the kaleidoscope rearranges the picture, presenting a vast throng gathered in one of those bare ravines to hear the hermit preach; for the word has been passed, by the salt merchants, that an eccentric but unusually stirring person is down there prophesying the speedy overthrow of existing authority and the advent of a celestial potentate; and hundreds have gone out to investigate. It is a miscellaneous crowd, as to personnel, but not without the distinction conferred by the presence of many well-known scholars, priests, and elders from the Holy City.

John the Baptist had nothing to lose by his audacity except his life, which he held lightly; and, in consequence, his addresses made up in candor all that they lacked in the customary courtesy shown to persons of high degree. One suspects the richness of John's vocabulary in the terminology of frankness when one reads that he saluted his distinguished auditors from

Jerusalem with such amenities as "Ye Generation of Vipers!" This matter is mentioned, in passing, to make sure we have this monastic figure in clear focus and understand his mood. The days of kowtowing to a snobbish priesthood and the self-contained Pharisee caste had been superseded by a new epoch. The language of entreaty was no longer necessary in dealing with these privileged people. One could afford to lay aside all prudence and speak one's mind. The priestly order had long been in the saddle, but Nemesis was waiting for it just around the corner; for a king was coming who would set things to rights!

The portrait John drew of this new king was an arresting sight. "The axe shall be laid at the foot of the tree!" "His fan is in his hand, and he will thoroughly purge his floor!" Long enough had the world been in the grip of predatory politics and equally unscrupulous priesthoods! The whole social order was built on monstrous injustices! Nothing short of divine judgment would effect the necessary reprisals and put the general scheme o' things in the grip of righteousness. The king would come with a new jurisprudential surgery that would drastically cure, even if it had to cauterize by fire, the malignant cancers of society.

One turns from this singularly interesting tableau with reluctance, but the steps in this story are too many to permit much tarrying at any particular phase of it. The narrative grows intensely dramatic as the scene of John's activities moves northward into the more settled region along the west bank of the Jordan River. Here one observes the augmented crowds, standing transfixed under the thunder blasts of the hermit's impassioned denunciation of the whole contemporaneous social structure. It is difficult to find, in all literature, examples of a more blistering contempt for every established institution. The great congregations paled under the hammer blows of the fearless recluse; and when he commanded them to seek what protection they might, from the wrath to come, by applying for citizenship in the new kingdom, they marched with him down into the turbid Jordan and were naturalized into John's spiritual commonwealth by the rite of baptism.

One afternoon there appeared in that vast throng a man who, when he asked for baptism, encountered the eye of the hermit, and held it fascinated. Here was a new type. John had seen all kinds. Every manner of repentant or frightened human had crowded into his audiences, and he had led to the river's brink all sorts of people, from the priest in his sacerdotal robes to the beggar in his filthy rags; but there was something written in this face that nobody else in all the world possessed. John knew that he himself did not have it. It was the new light of a social redemption, the redemption John longed for; but it was clearly a kindly light that sought comradeship, peace, and conciliation.

The hermit searched the face of the stranger. Here he had been pounding away, day after day, on the subject of divine vengeance, predicting calamities, announcing the inevitable arrival of a judge who would reconstruct society with an axe; and now, perhaps, there was a better way. In that face John saw the chasm between his own ideals and the ineffable glory of the perfect ideal as reflected here.

It may be presumed that no higher testimony has been offered concerning the majestic dignity resident in the bearing of Jesus than that which is implied in John's instant recognition of spiritual kingship in this man whose every feature, gesture, and tone, completely denied, down to the last detail, the picture the hermit had drawn of the coming king!

"I have baptized you with water," John had been shouting, to the penitent throng. "He will baptize you with fire!"

It was easily to be seen that this stranger was not the type that would baptize anybody with fire; or water, either. He seemed unconcerned about anything but idealism in its broader considerations.

"This is he!" said John to his breathless audience. "This is he of whom I spoke, the latchet of whose shoes I am unworthy to loose!"

Let us not forget, in our assembly of portraits to be hung in the gallery of the supermen, this portrait of the bronzed, seamed, fanatical hermit of the Jeshimon! Consider here the case of a mystic and monastic who for years has been shrieking up and down the dry wadies of the wilderness that a great and powerful judge would shortly come, fan in hand, to blow, all that was worthless out of the whole social order and consign such chaff to unquenchable flames; who would carry out the demands of an inexorable justice by laying the axe of divine retribution at the root of a debauched civilization. Consider, also, how this voice of "one crying in the wilderness" makes itself heard until all the country comes out to weep and pray, begging for admittance into the unique kingdom of the soul. Consider, further, the natural pride of success which must have stirred the heart of this brawny hermit when the thousands sought him in his remote retreat and hung eagerly upon his fiery words.

And now, in the very midst of a lurid description of the wrath to come, there arrives—not in the hot haste of an iconoclast, but with the leisurely stride of one seeking friends—a young man in peasant dress who, if the whole world were to be scoured for John's promised judge, would be the very last to qualify. It is at this point that the hermit rises to majestic proportions of wisdom and self-renunciation. "This is he!" It was the equivalent of saying: "Everything I have been telling you about the new king is incorrect. I told you he would come with axe and flail. I told you he would come in judgment. You see how little I knew. This man has not come in wrath; but—this is he!" If you are looking for any finer acts of self-abasement than this, you will find them in the career of only one other in all the world's history; and that other now stands at the hermit's side, requesting baptism.

After a short parley, for John feels himself unworthy to perform the rite and must be gently persuaded to do so, Jesus is formally inducted into the new social commonwealth of souls. He does not stop to debate whether it would be proper for him to join this order, seeing that the appeal in response to which the thousands had consecrated themselves was so far afield from the things he himself believed about the salvation of society. All that concerns Jesus at this moment is the obvious motive of John and his congregation. The world must be saved. If John's technique of salvation differs from the Nazarene's, that difference of process will not obscure the main fact that they both earnestly desired the same thing—social redemption.

One wonders what Jesus is going to do now. There seem to be several courses open. He has been formally presented to the congregation; he has been accepted and acclaimed by John. Perhaps he will deliver an inaugural address. He may say that doubtless John meant well enough when he talked about judgment, fire, flails, and axes, but that the new campaign of social reconstruction called for more effective methods than the old process of force and retribution. It is quite possible that Jesus debated with himself what he ought to do or say on this dramatic occasion. He may have been in doubt about the thing to say that would be at once true and courteous.

He said nothing. He walked slowly away toward the south. Everybody knew where he was going. There was nothing in that direction but the Jeshimon Wilderness. John had found his courage and faith down there, through years of lonely meditation and self-examination. It was in that forbidding spot that John had laid hold upon a great power, through his voluntary isolation. Jesus now resolves that he too will seek that retreat and examine his own spiritual credentials in the undisturbed stillness of the desert. It was the very highest tribute the Master could pay to the man who had presented him to a waiting world: to go directly from the impressive scene of his inauguration to the wilderness John had left. It was tantamount to saying to that crowd, "Before I can be your leader, I must gather strength where John found his!"

IV

It is to be hoped that the reader will not grow impatient with so much that is preliminary to a painstaking study of Jesus' experience in the Jeshimon Wilderness. As has been stated, we are not going to know anything about the miraculous element in the Master's life until we have seen him pass through this desert examination; and we cannot hope to understand the desert issue unless we know exactly how and why he went there.

The event we have just observed, along the Jordan's shore, is so profoundly significant, in its bearing upon Christianity's actual aims, that one wishes it might be better understood by the Church of our own day.

One would think that this impressive scene might have taught its own lesson to the world's energetic reformers in the ages which followed. But there has not been a generation since that day without its passionate iconoclasts who, to promote moral and spiritual progress, would gladly see a deluge of divine indignation come sweeping down upon a sinsick and blundering world. Always there is a group of white-hot reformers making religion odious and the very air hideous with their shouts of judgment impending; and this, too, in face of the fact that society is never moved forward an inch toward idealism by people who believe in the axe method. It has been definitely proved that Christianity's greatest gains have been made in periods when it suffered persecution, when its adherents were obliged to practice its golden tenets, not with the ornate splendor of liberty and prosperity, but in the common ways of private life. It has been shown also that Christianity has committed its worst blunders in the times of its apparent successes; when, by virtue of strong organization and intimate trafficking with political and economic powers, it has been able to wield the club and shout terrifying anathemas at its adversaries.

In the scene along the west bank of the Jordan, where John the Baptist has environed himself with enough influence to permit his daring to call the strongest institution in his land a race of snakes, without fear of retaliation from them or revolt on the part of the crowd, we have a fair sight of the kind of Christianity which today strolls confidently through the lobbies of legislative halls; which wires approval or condemnation to Senators; which stalks in the corridors of city buildings, asking questions; which steps in to adjudicate vexing issues between predatory organizations of labor and willfully unsympathetic combinations of capital. It bursts forth with a sudden flare of interest and zeal on behalf of the Lord's Day, and rigs up an organization that would close every candy shop, drug store and gasoline station on the first day of the week, not quite so much for sheer love of holiness, perhaps, as to sense the fine glow that comes with the exercise of authority.

For a few hours, maybe, it seems a wise and brave thing for some reforming movement, sailing under the orders of Christianity, to hold the club over the people's representatives in legislative assemblies, intimidate candidates to Congress, draw the fire of capitalists by encouraging the predatoriness of labor, and shout brave declarations of its intent to refuse to obey its country's call, in the event of an emergency inviting patriotic loyalty, but in the long run all such victories are worse than futile. Does anybody require a more spectacular example of Christianity with axe in hand than occurs in the history of the mediæval Church when it could command a king to wait barefoot in the snow before the papal gates, until St. Peter's lineal successor found it convenient to give him audience? Does anybody want a better proof of the way such a technique eventuates than the sight of great cathedrals now standing as museums and mausoleums, repudiated by the political states which once cowered under the dominion of a religious leadership that loved power for its own sake? Where once that type of world salvation shaped the very destinies of nations for a little while, its impressive seats and centers of strength maintained on a scale of lavish luxury, these ancient strongholds stand as monuments to a quite vanished glory. The sacristan will show you the relics for a couple of lire. Ten centuries from now our tourists may not have to travel so far to see glass-incased testimonials to the brief supremacy of Christianity's mailed fist.

John's mistake has been made many a time since his day. Surely there is enough evidence to be had in history to deter us from any further blunders of this particular type. We are greatly in need of this clear view of Jesus in his conference with the Baptist. He has listened to the program of redemption as outlined by the fiery prophet. He has stood quietly hearing the world excoriated and its speedy doom predicted. An infinite calm is on his brow. He is not quite so seriously disturbed about humanity's plight. He knows that there is much that is good, and much that is bad, and much that is merely misdirected. But if it is to be saved for some high purpose it will have to be saved by affection. It strikes him as poor business to be trampling down a green wheat field in an effort to pull up a few handfuls of weeds. He is willing to wait until autumn. The threshing floor is the place to determine values.

V

Jesus of Nazareth went down into the Jeshimon Wilderness with a few definite presuppositions in which he strongly believed, the chief of which may be briefly stated as follows: *The real man is not his body, but his soul.*

The Master proposed to stake his claim to the world's attention at the exact point of that declaration.

Of course, there was a wealth of divine logic back of this hypothesis. There was, for example, the theory of a man's divine sonship, which accounted for this supreme value of the soul. There was also the theory of God's providence which made it possible for a man to maintain his spiritual integrity and spiritual mastery in the face of the obvious claims of his body.

But, by whatever process of reasoning Jesus had

79

come by his belief, the final deduction was, The real man is not his body, but his soul. Jesus will now make an adventure to discover whether this statement would stand the test of experience. If not, there was little use to present it to other people as a working creed, no matter how idealistic it might sound in fair weather, immediately after luncheon.

It may be presumed that there were many events in the life of Jesus, of large significance to an adequate understanding of him, which his biographers did not record; but it is fortunate that we are permitted to see him in such a plight of desperate hunger that his feverish hallucinations drew the very stones at his feet into the shape of loaves.

The finest credentials any moral leader can present, who wishes to speak helpfully concerning the importance of ethical solutions for life's difficult emergencies, unquestionably reside in his own experience of severe adversity. The best authority on how to deal, wisely, righteously, and self-respectingly, with the problem of hunger is a hungry man. No others need apply. Society will never be much interested in what a rotund, modishly dressed parson thinks is the dignified and valorous way for poverty to behave itself.

Jesus goes to the wilderness glowing with the fine ardor of a prospector who has made a rich discovery of a valuable ore, and is *en route* with a nugget to the laboratory of an assayer. The whole world of men was accustomed to do its thinking about life in terms of, "I am a body that houses a soul." Jesus believes that there must be a fundamental revision of this doctrine to read, "I am a soul that utilizes a body."

It is to be doubted if the young Galilean could have found very much assistance in his thinking on this subject, outside his own meditations. One may deduce what help the religious leaders of the time might have offered to a man engaged in such high speculations when one recalls that the most serious points at issue among the priests concerned the depth of a hem on a cassock and the correct proportions of mint, anise, and cummon to be compounded as incense, and how many yards one might lawfully walk on the Sabbath Day. It was worse than discouraging to seek counsel of people who sat cross-legged all day in the inner chambers of the temple debating the various techniques of washing the cups and platters employed in sacrificial ceremonies.

Jesus realized that he had arrived at the tap root of the human dilemma. Was a man a body, going through life doing what best it could to save from impairment or destruction the soul that it housed, and occasionally regarded with pity or regret or misgivings because the hospitality offered it was so shabby? Or, was a man a soul, eternally marching forward, self-contained, and temporarily using a body as a bag of tools, while on this earthly pilgrimage? Let this problem be answered in favor of the soul's supremacy, and there was no question in the whole book of life that could not be answered promptly, joyfully, exultantly!

Not very many people, per hundred thousand, have ever faced an opportunity to discover exactly how they would behave in an emergency making a sudden and severe demand upon their spiritual power. To put it very concretely, not many people have had it put up to them to jump into the river, clothes and all, to try to save a life at the grave risk of their own. To do such a thing implies that one has oneself very well in hand; for, to the performance of it, the soul must be strong enough to pick up one's reluctant body and hurl it in. If the soul is in command of the body, the act may be performed. But the soul will not be able to do this if, in the ordinary discussions held in the court room of conscience, all litigation involving disagreements between the soul and the body are habitually settled in favor of the latter. If a man shall have arrived at that state where, whenever his senses cry out for something, he has to quiet their bawls by acceding to their vociferous demands, and has decided against the claims of his soul so frequently that it now speaks only in the dulcet whimper of unhopeful entreaty instead of the commanding voice of conscious power, he has good reasons to doubt whether, in some great moment, when a peak-load requirement is made of him, he is man enough to carry it without utter collapse.

Jesus had grown up in an atmosphere saturated with moral rules and regulations. The code of inhibitions seemed adequate to keep a man straight; but they were really inadequate because they were not addressed to the soul, but to the body. Every thou-shalt-not was spoken to the individual on the theory that he was a body unfortunately geared up with sensory demands inciting him to be predatory, lustful, murderous, covetous, vengeful, sacrilegious, unfilial, untruthful, and disloyal. Jesus was going to demonstrate, if possible, that once a man became fully possessed of the idea that he was a soul, a son of God, with enough resident spiritual power to command his body at all times and under all circumstances, he would be beyond the need of the code which warned against sins the soul could have no possible interest in committing.

A good test of the theory could be made by experimenting with the body's primary urge—hunger!

One needs not stop to inquire whether or not hunger is the world's gravest problem. The question answers itself. All the great migrations, evolutionary mutations, wars, reformations, revolutions, if dissected, will be traceable back to this problem of bread.

At the present hour efforts are made by the erotic to prove that the sex impulse is the chief motivation of life: but men who have fasted for prolonged periods testify against that theory. The first claim of human life is to keep alive. After it has contrived a way to keep itself alive, it considers the urge to reproduce itself. Jesus made the supreme test of his theory when he fasted. Now he could find out whether he was a soul giving orders to a body, or a body giving orders to a soul.

Jesus came through this severe test with the exultation that only they can understand who have put their souls to the supreme examination and have been victorious. Now he could do anything! Everything! His soul was in command! If he could do it, so could other men. He would go to them and tell his story. If they would believe it, and practice it, the world could be saved! Among all the great discoveries that men have made of titanic energies, this was the most important fact ever disclosed! Radiant, ecstatic, Jesus leaves the Jeshimon and starts for the Holy City. Doubtless he staggered with bodily weakness as he trudged along the road, his triumphant spirit goading his enfeebled body to spend its ebbing resources in the victorious march. However regretful he may have been to overtax the physical instruments of his life, it was a satisfaction that it was his body he pitied, and not his soul. Most men, in private meditation, were accustomed to say, "Soul, you have been quite seriously neglected and shamefully abused; but some day when I have met all the claims of my body I shall listen to what you seem to want to tell me."

Victorious! Now Jesus must give the world his secret. He will go directly to the place of densest population and tell the story.

VI

As the pale Galilean encountered the jostling pack of quarreling, gesticulating humanity in the market place hard by the temple area, it occurred to him that however valuable was the new truth he desired to teach, he had not yet devised an educational process for the proper presentation of it to other people.

His discovery was so real and vital, in his own mind, that it had not struck him there would be any difficulty in explaining it to others. Surely one needed only to announce a fact so sublime as this, and every man who heard it would drop his tools, his face alight with a brand-new joy, and exclaim, "Why hasn't some one thought of that before? Victory! At last! Now, we can all be happy! The poor as well as the rich! Every man a son of God, and in command of his own life! Accept it? How could a man afford to be without it?"

But, here, in the fierce competition of the market place, Jesus saw that it was going to be much more difficult to impart his new truth than it had been to discover it, even at the price its scientific demonstration had cost him. He wanted to be alone again, to think this problem over. He climbed to the balcony of the temple and surveyed the scene below. The issue before him was, How may I secure men's attention to my new gospel? He may have pictured himself walking up to a group of perspiring bargainers, under a market booth, and telling them that he had demonstrated to his own satisfaction that men do not live by bread alone; that they live by spiritual energies divinely communicated from an omnipotent Father; that all this competition, this haggling and dickering and quarreling, was unnecessary to life's fulfillment; that if their souls were put in command of their bodies, they need never have another care. How would they receive such a message? The roughest would elbow him aside with the crisp remark that he was crazy. If any gave him a kindly word, it would be because he had the look of a man who needed a square meal.

No, it was not going to be an easy task to make men see this new gospel as he saw it. Perhaps, if he could demonstrate his theory for them so they could have ocular proof of its validity, they might listen. Suppose he were to offer indisputable testimony as to what he thought of the claims of his body! Ah! he had it! He would leap from the top of the temple! He would shout until they looked up! He would announce that he was going to leap down among them, unhurt! They would wait, breathlessly, silently, for him to make good his promise. That would be a good way to win the favorable attention of a crowd; for crowds have a crowd mind that enjoys such spectacles. Of course, if there were only one man down there in the street, and one on the pinnacle of the temple were to shout, "I'm going to jump down!" the man in the street, no matter who he was, would instinctively reply, in a frightened voice: "Don't! I beg of you!

Wait! I'll be up at once!" But the crowd would be glad to see a man leap from the pinnacle of the temple. It would do nothing to hinder him.

Now that he had proved how insignificant were the claims of his body, he may as well introduce his theory to the crowd by proving what he thought on that subject. He would leap down among them.

It is doubtful if we have realized how fully these temptations of Jesus explain the exact motivation back of his gospel. Down in the wilderness, he refuses to work a miracle in behalf of his body. Up on the pinnacle of the temple, he refuses to work a miracle in contempt of his body. The facts of human life must be properly evaluated! While it was true that the soul must be placed in supreme command of the body, one had to remember that the good God had given the soul a body to be rightfully employed. If a man's eye was the only instrument which his soul could not master, he might be warranted in plucking it out. It would be wiser to go through life with one eye than a weak soul. But nobody had a right to play tricks with his body to astonish a crowd!

Jesus decides against the leap. He has just as good reasons for refusing to risk his body now as for refusing to satisfy his body a few hours earlier. What this zealous young prophet of light needs to do, first, is to get his gospel into proper drawing; to get it stabilized. It must not be an impracticable thing that the average man cannot hope to understand, much less practice.

The Nazarene came down the temple stairs. He would tell his story, not before an awe-stricken crowd, but to individuals. He would reveal his secret to some friend; the friend would tell another friend. The gospel would go forward by this process. It would take more time than the other technique, but this was the better way.

One hears of huge sums paid for artistic masterpieces, an occasional celebrated picture having sold for more than a hundred thousand dollars. I wonder what would be the monetary value put upon a stenographic report of the conversation Jesus had with Peter, sitting on the shore of the sea of Galilee, that afternoon when he told him the story of the soul-commanded life, into which no fear could enter so long as it kept the channels open to The Source.

VII

These experiences of Jesus, in the heart of the Jeshimon Wilderness and on the pinnacle of the temple, although registering his definite refusal to perform two miracles of a dramatic character, opened to the inspired Galilean new understanding of the problems confronting him.

We need look no further for the secret of that matchless compassion and sympathetic magnanimity toward all humanity, no matter how sinful or sorely distressed. At our present hour, when Christianity and civilization have become so indivisibly identical that altruism in its ministry to the needy is easier to practice than avoid, we may find it difficult to understand how unique and unprecedented was this sentiment when taught by the Nazarene.

One of the structural features of Hebrew ethics vigorously maintained that the relation of righteousness and material prosperity was as the relation of cause and effect. The greatest of the Jewish kings had written (though one doubts whether any king should offer counsel on this subject, seeing how poorly his circumstances equip him to pose as an authority on social science), "I have never seen the righteous forsaken, nor his seed begging bread." It may have been true that David had not seen piety in distress, but that may have been from lack of proper opportunities for observation. It is scarcely expected of a king that he shall know much about the conditions in which penury ekes out its miserable existence. One suspects it was easy for Solomon, who had bankrupted his kingdom to surround himself with luxuries, to compose wise saws for the poor, extolling the merits of a dish of bitter herbs eaten in contentment. However valuable such counsel, it might, with much better taste, have originated in some other quarter than the palace of the improvident Solomon.

But here is the old Hebrew ethics in a nutshell: The

godly are providentially cared for. Let a man delight in the law of the Lord, and whatsoever he doeth shall prosper! This was the Israelite's major premise! The godly shall prosper!

Jesus begins his ministry with the memory of his self-examination fresh in his mind. Had he wrought the suggested miracle in the Jeshimon, turning stones into bread to appease his hunger, the old hypothesis might have remained unchanged. The poor might have gone on indefinitely, wondering how they might raise more corn and cattle, and thus prove to themselves and their neighbors that Jehovah had at last considered them pious enough to be recognized with tangible rewards.

Had Jesus not made his discovery of the real sources of righteousness and happiness, the ancient idea might have persisted which was embedded in every ethical document of his people. Not a word had been written into their most cherished moral code which laid a single social obligation upon the rich to regard the plight of the poor. It was high crime to steal, but the silence is eloquent concerning any relief which the man of property might extend to desperate poverty in order that it might not be tempted to appropriate the rich man's goods. It is not without significance that this hallowed decalogue should have reached its climax in an itemized list of the properties which a man must not covet. It was not enough that the poor man should not steal; he must refrain even from looking wistfully upon the comforts of the rich.

Jesus has a new message for the poor. He has demonstrated, in the wilderness, that the life is more than meat! Every man has enough inner spiritual resources to make him happy without houses and lands. A new wealth has been discovered which provides its own insurance, a wealth which neither moth nor rust can destroy, nor thieves break through and steal.

It was the refusal to ask for divine intervention to provide him with food that furnished the motivation for the Beatitudes. Now, for the first time, the hitherto unnoticed and unrewarded of God's children were to receive tidings of a new happiness to be found through contacts with their Father.

Under the terms of this new gospel, the meek would inherit the earth, the pure in heart would see God, the mourners would find a source of comfort, and the kingdom of heaven would be theirs whom the world had persecuted and reviled. Let a man's soul be in command, and he was rich. His treasure would reside eternally in his heart.

CHAPTER FIVE

THE TRANSFORMING PRESENCE

I

THEY still show you the stone pots, at Cana in Galilee, which Jesus ordered filled to the brim with water, prefatory to enacting the miracle which supplied a wedding feast with wine—such wine as was not common in humble Galilean homes, even on occasions of such vast import as a wedding. Of course the little house is still there, and the benches where the guests sat. Such proofs as the East conventionally offers pious pilgrims, as a pledge that its wonder tales are authentic, are not lacking at Cana. But even this wealth of material evidence need not deter us from making a reverent inquiry into this story—not with the intent of picking flaws, but seeking light.

This first miracle was performed in Cana, a little town only a few miles from Nazareth, where Jesus lived. It is said to have been wrought in the presence of a numerous company of guests. Whatever might, later, be remembered of the miraculous deeds of Jesus, it is reasonably safe to presume that the first miracle would attract a very great deal of attention. All of the gospel writers attach much importance to the early days of Jesus' ministry. Mark knows about the Nazarene's journey to John for baptism, knows about the first sermon preached in a little synagogue, knows all about the first conversation of the Master with Peter and Andrew along the seashore, but does not know anything about this first miracle. Matthew begins his narrative back in Bethlehem, loads his introduction with nativity incidents, and repeats all the stories afloat concerning Jesus' infancy; makes a fresh start and tells about the family life in Nazareth; recites the story of Jesus' baptism, his experiences in the wilderness, the recruiting of his disciples, and his appearance in Capernaum, hard by, to begin his teaching ministry; but Matthew knows nothing about this first miracle. Luke, also rich in nativity lore, handles the story of Jesus' early days in the ministry with painstaking detail; the temptations, the prompt return to Galilee, the first sermon, and what that sermon was about, and the effect it had upon the congregation; but Luke has no word for us about the first miracle. One thinks Mark might have mentioned it, for he is said to have received most of the data for his book from Peter, who was present at the wedding and should have been able to recall the event.

No one of the synoptists reports this first miracle, and the reader is eager to know why; for, seeing it is alleged to have happened in the immediate neighborhood and within that group of weeks which the gospels handle with such a richness of incidental detail, it seems doubtful if these narrators merely forgot to mention the strange occurrence. One thinks the historian would be almost obliged to step out of his way to avoid the inclusion of this story into his book, so conspicuously would it stand out against the uneventful background of casual talks with fishermen and sermons preached in village chapels.

May one make doubly sure, before we go any farther, that we are not now engaged in the doubtful enterprise of attempting to demolish the record of a miracle? Were there not, back of this investigation, a motive to discover a larger fact, concealed between the lines and spiritually implied in the story, we would better join the ranks of those who accept the narrative as a baffling mystery, and let it go at that. But there is a really tremendous story here, and it is our right to lay hold upon it, even if, to do so, we are obliged to clear away a few of the obvious difficulties clouding it.

Let us take a hasty glance at John's story of the event at Cana. Jesus is a guest at a wedding. His disciples have come with him. Seeing he lived close by and was likely invited because of long acquaintance with the families involved, and seeing also that his disciples had been recruited, more or less at random, as he strolled about through Galilee, these new friends of the Master's were probably invited not because they were known by the host, but solely because they were following Jesus.

Early in the feast the wine gave out. This was a

serious breach of hospitality. In this humble home frugality had to be considered somewhat, even on the occasion of a wedding. They had provided what they thought would be sufficient. Then comes Jesus, their Nazarene friend, accompanied by a full dozen robust and able-bodied companions. So the wine gave out.

Jesus retires quietly to the little patio outside, collects all the empty stone jars available, orders the servants to fill them with water, and presently the toastmaster is inquiring where this remarkable vintage came from, for it was customary to serve one's finest wine first.

The student of psychology criticizes the story on the ground that the people in it do not behave as people customarily act on occasions when some uncanny mystery projects itself into the quiet of normal life. The servants do as they were bidden. They fill the stone jars with water. The water turns to wine. The servants dip it out and serve it without comment, as nonchalantly as if this sort of thing were all in the day's work. The psychologist insists that the story would be improved at this point if one servant had fainted, another had shrieked, another had fled, and the entire wedding party had gathered about the stone jars, pale, trembling, and mentally disheveled. Be all that as it may. Our query does not reside in that quarter. It is not expected that all the details shall have come to us in the exact sequence of their happening. Our query does not concern the *how* of it, but the *why* of it!

Jesus has just returned from the Jeshimon Wilderness where he had met and solved a serious economic problem in the light of a great spiritual discovery. Fainting with hunger, he had been tempted to turn stones into bread. We are not informed whether or not he had the power to turn stones into bread, for he makes no effort to do so. Let us say that he possessed the power. Had he tried to do it and failed, that would have made a sorry tale indeed. But had he tried to do it and succeeded, that would have been little short of a tragedy. There could have been no gospel, after that.

What a picture, indeed, that would have made, of one who had hoped to put men's souls in tune with the Infinite; to show them how much greater was the splendor of the spirit than slavery to the defects and demands of the body! What a picture! The world's Light, Life, Hope, Truth, and Way calmly munching some food that he had created in absolute defiance of his hypothesis that the life is more than meat!

As we have seen, Jesus comes forth from that desert radiant over his great discovery that the soul could command physical appetites. Men do not live by bread. Henceforth Jesus can proceed unhampered by the demands of his body. Indeed, he is so infatuated with his new thought of the inferiority of his body that he is tempted to risk leaping from the balcony of the temple just to show the quarreling pack in the market place below how little the body mattered, as compared with the importance of the soul. Fresh from that experience of demoting bread from its erstwhile place of consequence as the chief consideration in men's esteem, Jesus goes back to Galilee to teach his new discovery; and the first thing he does after refusing to turn stones into bread on the ground that it was such things that the heathen seek, proceeds, in the face of that new life-giving theory, to turn water into wine, thus forgetting everything he had learned, at so great cost, in the Jeshimon!

It is this feature of the literal story of the miracle at Cana that is practically insurmountable. If accepted exactly as it stands, it leaves one bereft of all the high spiritual culture so radiantly portrayed in that tremendously soul-searching wisdom of the wilderness experience! Here you have, not a redeemer transforming dull and uncourageous souls, enslaved to their physical appetites, into valorous heroes, capable of demonstrating how much more powerful is the spirit than the flesh, but a mere magician, performing a miracle to tickle the palates of a dinner party. If this story is literally correct and must be accepted at its face value, then you must run a blue pencil through a very great deal of the Sermon on the Mount.

II

Having now gazed quite long enough at the knotted side of this curious tapestry, let us turn it over and look at the vital features of the picture. It is to be hoped we can see something of the beauty that resides here; for to miss the important fact allegorically presented in the second chapter of John's gospel is to have passed carelessly by one of the most transcendently lovely bits in the whole New Testament literature.

It is assumed the reader knows that Matthew, Mark, and Luke approach the story of Jesus from practically the same angle and deal with it on the same terms, which accounts for their being called the "synoptic" gospels.

The gospel of John, written at a much later date, long after all the first-hand witnesses of the career of Christ had passed away, stands quite alone, apart from the other evangelical documents, as to style, technique, approach, mission, and motive. Where Mark is offering a photograph, John is painting an impressionistic portrait. Where Luke is telling a story, John is writing a poem. Where Matthew is composing a biography, John is creating an oratorio.

When you open the book of John you should keep it in mind that you are expected to be in much the same mood as when you begin Milton's "Paradise Lost," or the immortal work of Dante. John proposes to dramatize the life of Christ, staging it, as it were, in a series of startlingly stirring tableaux. Approach it as if you were in a theater. The curtains part. A chronicler, ageless, timeless, clad in the simple tunic and sandals of life untortured by artifice, steps forth and in the majestic tones of one belonging rather to the eternal years than to any particular era, race, or country, begins to intone the sonorous phrases which for elegance of diction and height of spiritual fervor are unequaled in all the lore of all the ages. "In the beginning was the Logos"—the Logos, science of life; the all-knowledge of all-power; that gripping, untranslatable word whence we have deduced our suffix "ology," which makes sociology the science of the social order; geology, the science of the earth; anthropology, the science of mankind. "In the beginning was the Logos, and the Logos was with God, and the Logos was God. In him was life, and the life was the light of men. And the light shineth in darkness, and the darkness could not enshroud it."

The chronicler retreats; the curtains fall; the prologue to the play is ended. There is a pause, and presently the first scene comes on—a tableau of the baptism by the River Jordan. The curtains close, opening again on the calling of the disciples. And now the curtains part to disclose the incident with which we are directly concerned.

The text says, "And the third day, there was a marriage in Cana of Galilee." We are not asked to take critical account of John's method of keeping the calendar. He has already started one paragraph with, "And the next day"; and another with, "And again the next day"; and another with, "The day following," previous to this "third day." John does not mean a third *day,* but a third *picture!* For, you see, these are idealistic portraits, tableaux. John is not writing a history, but a great prose poem, dealing with broad impressions. Many weeks of Jesus' ministry have passed; but in the poem it is only the third day.

Jesus was invited to a wedding. It was the most natural thing in the world that he should have been asked and that he should have accepted the invitation. It is easy to understand how he asked his hostess to enlarge the invitation to include his friends. Under these circumstances, it is natural that the supply of wine should have been exhausted. But it is the most inconceivable situation that Jesus would have tried to remedy that predicament by an appeal to God for supernal aid.

No; in the after days, long after Jesus had been put to death by a jealous and predatory priesthood and the little bands of Christians were meeting under cover and by stealth to renew their courage and confidence in the glow of their mutual faith, it was doubtless remembered, by some one who had attended that wedding, that Jesus had come to the feast. Ah, what a day that was! It was in a home of poverty, but the family were doing their honest best to put on a brave front and give their precious girl the very finest wedding party they could contrive to finance. Unexpected guests, however, placed just enough extra load on this precarious program of hospitality to topple it. Their slender resources weren't equal to the demand. But with Jesus there, it was as if the water they drank had turned to wine.

And then the story began to pass along. Every time it was told about an evening camp fire it took on incident and detail and episode. Presently there was a definite narrative. John catches at it as a gorgeously beautiful, typical setting for the portrait he wishes to draw of *the transforming power of Jesus' presence!*

It is a picture unsurpassed in charming imagery. Jesus comes to a frugal feast in a humble home, and immediately it is as if their water had become wine. Of course, the minstrel could be depended upon to embellish the story. That's what minstrels are for; and perhaps the beautiful little poem would never have reached us at all, at this long distance in years and miles, if it had not been floated down the current of the centuries on this allegorical raft with so many water pots on board, and so much mysterious conversation between Jesus and his mother, his mother and the servants, the servants and the guests. We must permit the minstrel to sing his song, without asking him to parse it.

Surely he is a very unfortunate reader of this epic who gets himself so distracted by all these stone water pots, and strange commands, and the various properties of this miracle tale, that he misses the real and only point at issue, which is, after all's said that can be said either by the literalist or the liberalist, the simple fact that Jesus bears a transforming power, that he turns water into wine, frowns into smiles, whimpers of fear into anthems of hope, deserts into gardens, and sin-blistered souls into valorous saints, by the catalyzing alchemy of a selfless love.

III

This transforming power, whereby Jesus once wrought a miracle at a banquet table, and still works miracles for all who have the spiritual vision to see and understand his wonders, is a power that may be ours for the asking. When the Master said, of his deeds, "Greater works than these shall ye do," he must have considered this transformation act as one of the very simplest in the whole category of wonders. Perhaps John presented it as a typical "first" miracle because it would make a very good experiment for the Christian to begin on.

In some form or another, this transforming miracle is performed every day in our own experience. Sometimes the miracles of transformation that we effect are not very satisfactory; easy enough to do, but rather hard on the customers. You can come to the breakfast table, for example, any time you like, after a restless night of indigestion or a tussling with yesterday's business perplexities or of having it out with your conscience, and by a few well-aimed remarks, loaded with sharp slugs of satire and propelled by a bad temper, work a miracle there for everyone about the family board, turning their toast into ashes, their bacon into leather, their butter into motor grease, their marmalade into glue, and their coffee into poison. I know it can be done, for I've done it!

Not quite so easy, but vastly more pleasant, is the exercise of a transforming power that makes everything taste better than it was originally meant to. I presume the real question at issue is: Since we are all possessed, to greater or less degrees, with this transforming capacity, what manner of miracles are we performing?

I am sure I do not know just how hard it would be to turn stones into bread, for, to the best of my information, it has never been done; but I know that bread can be turned into stones, for I have sat at tables where it was done and where people wept in secret afterward because it was done. It depends considerably on one's habitual view of life—whether one believes that the world is on the way up and on, or on the way down and out—whether one is more of a success at turning water into wine than turning wine into water.

John, the Beloved, never intended this story of his to be made a battleground for tempestuous saints who never see farther into it than "Do you, or don't you, believe it?" John would have been the first to protest that it was not for this that he had offered this lovely poem. All John wants to disclose is divine love in action. He does it by the pictorial method. The only question he wants raised is: How does your score stand, Christian, in working transformations? Are you getting good results?

Perhaps, if we were to review the list of our recent miracles of transformation, we might be chagrined to observe that we have been changing things, mostly, to their very decided unimprovement. Our journal of wonders records the item that the other day we met a man on the street who was wearing a smile, and when we left him he was wearing a scowl. Quite a charming little miracle, that.

We note, by our diary, that we came into a group of three whose voices were vibrant with the full enjoyment of life, and before we had been there five minutes these same voices were high-pitched and querulous as they laid some absent friend's reputation on the table and dissected it to its last shivering shred. We came into a meeting that was full of zeal and hope for some difficult but necessary achievement, and said some words over it that turned the affair into a dismal farce, so that the promises people were making flattened out into excuses and protests.

It all depends upon one's point of view whether one turns things into better or worse things than they were before.

The one ethereally beautiful thing about Jesus' transforming touch is that wherever he goes things change for the better. His gospel of love invades an island, and presently the people's clothes are mended, their food is more appetizing, their music is more melodious. He turns weeds into flowers. No reason why we should be so dull as to make a great spectacular feat of it with a lot of magic, just to make him seem entirely different from ourselves in capacity, when he so definitely states that he desires nothing else than to be one of us and with us and for us.

He can and does change dog fennel into daisies, and it is a miracle, if you like that word; but there is no necromancy about it. You can do it yourself if you try. Jesus can make a very homely face beautiful. He can and does make the meek legatees of everything in the world that is worth having. He makes the pure in heart so keen-sighted they can see God. He turns griefs into spiritual disciplines, so that they who mourn are possessed of an enduring comfort. And the grace that was in his soul, caught up and translated into our daily lives, gives us, also, this miracle-working power. By that grace we establish ourselves in the confidence of our friends, so that they know, when they see us coming, that whatever gets transformed into something other than it was, it will not be changed, at our behest, into anything worse than it was.

By that grace which was and is in Christ we can work transforming wonders on our own hearts, enriching them until they are fortified against all the ills and disappointments to which we are exposed. This gift is ours to possess not only here, but borne along into the life beyond, where we "may be the cup of strength to other souls in some great agony, and the sweet presence of a good diffused. So shall we join the choir invisible, whose music is the gladness of the world."

CHAPTER SIX

A GREAT CALM

I

HOW to live without fear: let this problem be solved, and all other problems of life are insignificant. The secret of the mastery of fear is understanding, and the road to understanding is faith. This is the thesis of the most dramatic story recorded of Jesus' supernormal power to deal with men's terrors.

In the opinion of the normal mind nothing is so thoroughly admirable as valor, that capacity of the human spirit which enables men to meet danger with conscious strength of courage.

Every man knows by experience that he is good for certain exactions laid upon his bravery. He has been through minor accidents without experiencing mental stampede. He has encountered specific dangers without serious loss of self-control. But he knows there are plenty of things that he is afraid of, and he wishes this were not so. He covets the ability to say to himself that he is living his life above the reach of fear. It is exactly as if he drove a little car which had plenty of power for the straight-away and smooth roads, but held out no promise of capacity to climb a hill. He wants to be able to go where he likes, in all weathers.

It may be believed that all timidity and cowardice can be definitely traced back to a fallacy in our general philosophy of life. This sophistry, which sends the vast majority of people through all their days anxious, harried, worried, may be briefly comprehended by the untruth, "A man must live." The hypothesis hasn't a leg to stand on. The only absolutely certain fact about our life is that we are mortal. Let a man devote all his energies to the business of keeping alive; detouring, at great inconvenience, around every situation that might involve hazard; refraining from participation in many a desirable activity because it holds an element of risk; and, after having shielded himself as he may, the ultimate hour strikes when all that he can do to save himself is absurdly futile.

With what disappointment and chagrin must a man watch his vitality slowly oozing out of him, who had concentrated his best efforts upon the enterprise of remaining here. All his life he had premised every act upon "A man must live." On no account must he brave inclement weather, for he might "catch cold"; the result might be pneumonia. He had wished to go abroad and view the historic spots of the Old World, but the boat might go down. Once he had strongly longed for the right to go downstairs and investigate a strange disturbance that sounded like rattling silver in the dining room, but it might have put him into an encounter with a marauder.

And now that he has consistently limited his knowledge, restricted his experiences, denied himself pleasures, and sacrificed the respect of his own household, to pay toll to his fears, he learns that, today, in the fastness of his own rocking-chair, apparently safe from all alarms, there is a hand reaching for him from which he cannot hide. His fundamental philosophy of life was incorrect. It is not true that a man must live. Quite to the contrary, it is definitely certain that a man must die.

If it were true that one might conserve one's earthly life and remain here always, provided there were no accidents or illness to cut short his tenure, this "a man must live" philosophy might admit of some debate. It could be pointed out that it is a man's proper destiny to be an earthling forever. To risk hazards which might jeopardize that destiny would be reprehensible. But when it is a fixed, immutable law that it is not life but death which carries the guaranty of one's future, persons who devote any considerable amount of time or talent to the enterprise of keeping alive are merely engaged in a controversy with the clock.

The most alluring offer which Jesus holds out to those who accept his code of living is the promise of an insured valor. He does not try to make men contented with some specific form of protection that reduces certain risks and thus clears the way of obstacles on a given path. He prescribes a general formula for the complete abrogation of all fears.

His own valor was no pumped-up courage, arrived at by a specific resolution to make a risk in a given situation, but a steady state of mind in which fear had no standing whatsoever. He had come by it through a constant spiritual contact with the Father who controlled all the energies of the universe. It was a tremendously reassuring thought that his life was in the hands of the Supreme Arbiter. It was of little consequence to him what happened to his body, for the only enduring fact about him was his soul. Having come to that conclusion, he was not put to it to decide what type of dangers might with impunity be dared and what type of dangers must by all means be avoided. All jeopardies were alike to him in that no one of them had any weight. Sooner or later he and every other man would put down the working tools of earthly existence. This was inevitable. In the last analysis of our life, all that remained was the spirit. It was decidedly important that a man take such pains to safeguard the well-being of his soul that when the day came for him to go on into a state of life where he would be nothing more, less, or else than a soul, he could present himself without fear or shame.

If it had not been so desperately tragic, it would have been ridiculous, the way most people lived. As if it were not absurd enough to be devoting an exorbitant amount of their time and energy to answering such petty questions as "What shall we eat?" and "What shall we drink?" about all that was left of their ambition went into worry over "What shall we put on?"

Solomon, widely celebrated as a wise man, had beggared a kingdom in his efforts to outdo all his royal contemporaries in the ornateness of his haberdashery, and, having reduced his realm to penury and revolution in his zeal to array himself and his court in extravagant finery, he was a shabby thing compared with a wild lily growing without cultivation in the field —a lily that had never given a thought to its appearance.

Let Solomon the wise spend all forenoon in a perfumed bath and all afternoon in the hands of expert masseurs, so that he may be made very, very beautiful; let Solomon the regal load himself with silks and jewels; the day will come when no amount of raiment, however costly—even though the price of it should ruin his kingdom—can make Solomon look pretty any more. Many a time Solomon had discarded some expensive suit on the ground that he was weary of it and wished never to see it again, and the gaudy outfit was folded carefully by the flunkies, and put away; but how surpassing beautiful was that discarded clothing as compared with the repulsive thing that Solomon was, in death—a stiff, ashen-colored, ugly lump of clay. So this was the thing, then, that the wisest man in the world had bankrupted a kingdom for—this thing that could not achieve the dignity of an outworn garment, but must be buried deeply out of sight because it was obnoxious. Let a man begin thinking about his precious body in such terms, and he has cleared the way for a little honest thinking about his soul.

So completely had Jesus devoted himself to his hypothesis of soul supremacy, that only the spirit had for him a real and significant existence. He was utterly indifferent to all forces which menaced his body. The result of such thinking was the complete mastery of fear. Nor was this a unique gift of valor which only a Christ could possess and exercise. Jesus said that any man could make this philosophy of life his own, and that any man who held this philosophy of life would live above the dominion of fear. He marveled that any man could gain the consent of his own mind to live a whole life of worry and dread when he might face every danger calmly and open-eyed.

One of the finest contributions which the Master offered to the world's thought on this subject is presented in the record of his attitude during a storm at sea. The story needs to be reviewed, from time to time, to hearten people who toss about bewilderedly upon waves too rough to be dealt with by natural means.

II

A little party of Galileans are having a bad night on their erratic inland sea. It was only a small body of water, but whimsical of mood and uncertain of temper. The disciples are at their wits' end. Their boat has shipped all the water she can take. The wind howls through the torn rigging and the waves wash over the rail. Jesus sleeps. He was not feigning sleep. He was serenely unconscious. His philosophy of life which held that he was safe in his Father's world and in the fastness of his Father's love had become so deeply grounded in his permanent self that there was no room in him for fears.

His disciples, however, were greatly alarmed. They roused their Master with a wail of complaint. Was it nothing to him that they were in jeopardy of their lives? How much did he care? Here they were, full to the gunwale with water, and the tiller swept overboard, and everybody frightened almost to death; and Jesus is asleep. They shook him by the shoulder. "Master! Carest thou not that we perish?" It was not precisely the approach that suppliants should make to one who, they think, might offer a remedy for their predicament. Only one man on board who had the capacity to do anything in this emergency; and here the helpless crew waits until everything was either overboard or waterlogged, belatedly accosting him with: "Get up! We're going down! And much you seem to care!"

One sees it all enacted, again and again. Much he cares, indeed! Much he cares about me! Everything I had is gone. That which I most dearly loved—gone.

Hopes blasted; sky overcast; sails tattered; masts splintered; rudder lost. Much he cares about me. Much he cares about anybody. We're mere atoms, adrift in an unfriendly world of cruel storms!

We have the record of three gospels for it that Jesus arose and spoke to the storm; that it obeyed him; that there was a great calm. The minor incidents in the three narratives differ slightly, but all agree that Jesus stilled the storm. Perhaps that is all we need know about it for our own use. Jesus spoke, and there was a great calm.

The ultra-conservative is eager to have the story accepted literally. To his mind, unless one believes all of it, exactly as it stands, one does not believe enough. But our contention is that if one stops with merely believing what appears on the surface of the text, one has not believed enough to make the incident of eternal value to the storm-tossed.

An inquiring mind sees but little achieved if, to take the story literally, Jesus merely speaks to the winds and waves. Surely he knew it was not the fault of these waves that they were rolling up such a vast deal of discomfort and terror for these helpless fishermen. There was no use talking to these insensate waves about it. As well chide the lava when a volcano erupts. What is a wave, after all, but so much water tossed up by a gale? And what is a gale but so much velocity of wind propelled by thermal conditions existing a thousand miles away, perhaps?

Suppose we accept the bare narrative with slavish literalness, forgetting how these people always spoke pictorially, and concede that Jesus actually spoke to the winds and waves. What would be the net result of that act? Did the Sea of Galilee become any more easily navigable, thereafter? It did not. Did the event add anything to the science of navigation? Not a bit. Did the disciples know any more about how to handle a boat in rough water than they had known before? Not at all.

The very best we can say of it, if all we can see in the literal text is that here is a Miracle Man finding a way out of an emergency for himself and his party, by doing something nobody else had ever done or could ever do. The benefit conferred is good for that date and place only. A thousand ships will go down, through the succeeding ages, carrying their shrieking cargoes of men, women, and children to the slime of the ocean floor; but Jesus' great secret will be safe. His reputation as the world's supreme wonder worker will be secure. He can be forever referred to as the only man who ever spoke to a storm in tones of command.

The story, viewed thus, leaves us cold. We try to understand the beauty and power of it, but the facts lay a heavy hand upon the endeavors of our loyal discipleship to rise exultantly in praise of a type of mercy which is so narrowly restricted to a given time and place. We attempt to key up to the proper pitch of admiration over the sight of a raised hand that demands silence and the sound of a majestic voice that demands peace; but are palsied with the thought that all the believing world gets out of it is the record of a magician doing a thing that can never be done again; spending that one unique outburst of divine power to quiet a storm on a little lake in an obscure country on the other side of the earth, after which that lake, and all the other lakes in all the other countries, and all the oceans of all the world, are, next night, as dangerous as ever; the winds as boisterous as ever; and never again, while humanity lives, will the act of love and mercy be repeated. It fails to satisfy. Indeed, it not only fails to satisfy, but it leaves a bad taste; it distorts the portrait of the Saviour; it warps, out of drawing, the figure of him who had come to rescue men from their fears by proposing measures of trust and confidence guaranteed to produce an inextinguishable human valor.

But there was a very real miracle performed that night! In the midst of a perplexity which had completely stampeded his disciples, Jesus spoke. So instantaneous was the reassurance of his voice, projected from a faith-controlled life, all fear vanished from the wildly beating hearts of his timid retinue. It was as if he had magically silenced the winds and smoothed the waves! He spoke! His words proceeded from a soul forever kept and sustained in the tranquil consciousness of a Father's providence. He spoke out of a faith so much more powerful than any storm that the very tones of his voice produced a great calm.

But where was this great calm needed? Where else but in the tumultous hearts of these frightened men? He turns to them, saying, "Why are ye afraid?" I think we must bear down heavily here on the word "ye." It went without saying that many men could be expected to crumple under the noise and fury of a storm. It had always been so. Storms were very affrighting to people who had no inner power and peace sufficiently grounded to warrant their walking calmly and with assurance through any difficulty that might arise. But it was different with these men in this little boat. Day after day the Master had been schooling them in all the implications of his new discovery. Life could be absolutely self-contained! Nothing could ever happen that need upset one's spiritual equilibrium.

Sometimes it appeared that the little band of Galileans, seated on a hill slope, of a late afternoon, listening breathlessly to Jesus' proffer of a new kind of power that could be exercised in all emergencies—sometimes it seemed that they had indeed made this faith their own. They saw the full beauty of it. They were eager to experiment with their wonderful gift. By faith they could overcome the world!

And now, in this predicament on the little sea, the first really testing strain is laid on. It will be good for them to face one another in a storm, after their many eloquent and sincere expressions of faith in a providence entirely capable of seeing them through every emergency.

For this test of their new courage had not come upon them while they were still novitiates, lacking instruction in the power and promise of the Jesus-faith. Why, only this afternoon, an address by the Master to a vast multitude had been so stirring and effective that men had come forward to profess their understanding and acceptance of his way of life. One had promised to join Jesus' company as soon as he had buried his father. Another had shouted, in an outburst of enthusiasm, "Master, I will follow thee whithersoever thou goest!" The disciples had had an opportunity to grasp the significance of the new teaching. Doubtless they thought they had the gospel well in hand. But tonight they forget their new philosophy. Their scattered thoughts, as the wind raked the little boat and the waves rolled over them, slipped into the old grooves worn deep with long years of timidity and self-protection. Jesus expresses surprise. He would not have been surprised to see almost any other dozen men of his acquaintance wailing in fear of a storm; but, "How is it that *ye* have no faith?"

What is it that *you* need ever be afraid of? One can understand how persons who have had no chance to learn the deeper meaning of life, and for whom there have been but few spiritual privileges—one understands how they will experience panic, lose their heads, go into hysterics, and rail at an unfriendly fate; but what are *you* afraid of?

You have given up everything humanly dear to follow this new program of life. You have left your homes; you sleep out-of-doors; you occasionally go hungry. There are many who revile you and speak disrespectfully of you. The world is full of pleasures which you have renounced. You have done all this because you wished to live without fear. *Now look at you!*

There was a great calm. There was a calm in the storm. Jesus does not try to save men from storms, but in storms. Experienced mariners never attempt to drive their ships up on dry land to escape a tempest at sea. Land is the very last and worst solution of their problem. Their task is to try to keep the ship seaworthy in the sea.

As a stiller of storms on seas, Jesus has made no contribution to the world's safety. He has done nothing and does nothing to the weather or the waves or the winds; but he did and does address the tempests of anxiety and fear in human hearts.

Jesus never asks to navigate your boat. He keeps his hand off the tiller and volunteers no suggestions. It is your boat. He is a passenger, and it is as if he slept serenely in his berth. You can forget that he is on board. Many people do. Sometimes, when the storm has completely outwitted them, they remember that he is with them, and rush to him with the whimper, "We're sinking; and you don't care!"

Jesus is aboard and ready to speak peace—not to the howling wind and roaring waves. It's not the wind and waves that need divine attention. It is *you!* The real storm is inside of *you!* The tempest that endangers is inside of *you!* Where the great calm must come is inside of *you!*

III

Whoever feels that this interpretation of the miracle wrought in the storm on Galilee subtracts from the majesty of Jesus' power, should reflect that we not only have safeguarded the essential fact of that event on the little sea, but have added a longer reach to the arm extended over those tossing waves. Now we have all we had before, plus the assurance that this act of producing peace in the midst of a storm can be effected by anyone who lives a faith-controlled life.

Does one rise to protest that the Scriptures definitely state certain circumstances and incidents relating to this event, deliberately and willfully ignored in our interpretation, the truthful reply is that we have temporarily excluded from the picture everything that might obscure the main issue. That main issue is that Jesus stilled the storm. Our hypothesis is that the storm was in the hearts of these terrorized men. When the great calm came, it was they who experienced that calm.

The waves did not know whether they were calm, or not. The waves had had no sense of being disturbed. The wind had been unaware of any need for supernormal intervention. Let peace come to the sea, and it will be all the same to the sea as when tumult is on.

No, you haven't lost your miracle; unless, of course, you are merely trying to safeguard the integrity of magic! But the trouble about insisting upon mere magic is that while it surprises, stuns, and mystifies, it has nothing to teach us. The prestidigitator pulls a rabbit out of a hat, and smiles at his client's bewilderment. He does not explain how he has done the feat; nor can he explain why he has done it, except for the sheer purpose of astounding. Let it be supposed that in an outburst of generosity he volunteers to reveal his secret. He goes through his motions very slowly; omits the tricks which had previously distracted the attention of the audience; exhibits the apparatus necessary to the act—and now it is all clear enough. With a little practice, anybody can do it, perhaps.

But why? If anybody else ever does it, he will do it with the same motive that inspired the magician— namely, to astound and mystify! As for the actual value of the intrinsic act of producing a rabbit from a hat, what is the good of that? Is it to be recommended that persons seeking rabbits shall look for them in hats? No; all that the magician hopes to accomplish is the bewilderment and mystification of his clients. This is all that magic has ever tried to do, whenever and wherever it has operated. Its motive is to astound through deception and illusion. Are you willing to see Jesus playing that rôle? Is he merely bent on astonishing people? Is he doing tricks? Do you like to see him doing things that merely bewilder?

Let us find it more consistent to believe that Jesus, far from wishing to add bewilderment and mystification to life—already sufficiently difficult to understand—was concerned chiefly with an endeavor to clear up mysteries, and bring peace into men's souls.

One presumes that he is still surprised over the curious lack of orderliness and consistency in the minds of his followers. They talk much of his saving grace; they build costly churches to house the agencies which teach his great discovery of what an energetic faith can do in the life of man; they cut themselves off from many a transient pleasure, and cheerfully make sacrifices to advance what they refer to as Jesus' "kingdom."

And all they get out of it is the promise that they can live without worry or fear. Of course, that is everything—but that is what they hope to achieve; just that; nothing less or else than that. Unless, in times of storm, they are able to realize this promised peace, they get nothing. If they have it, they have everything; if they do not have it, they have nothing.

What are we afraid of? How is it that we, with all that we have seen and heard and declared of God's providence in the world—how is it that *we* have no faith?

We can have it! We, too, can still storms! When the confidence that gave serenity to the soul of Jesus shall have become ours, there will arrive in our lives the calmness of the unafraid, the spiritual splendor of the unbound, the mental majesty of an overcoming faith, and the peace that surpasses all understanding.

CHAPTER SEVEN

DESERT BREAD

I

ONE of the most spectacular disclosures of Jesus' supernormal power is recorded in the story commonly known as the multiplication of the loaves and fishes. Whether this event means more to us, today, when interpreted as a multiplication of food or as a division of food, under the influence of a divine ideal, is clearly the thesis of our present study.

A great deal of inexcusably unnecessary hunger was on display in the land where Jesus lived. Beggars lay literally starving to death at rich men's doors. Pitiful frugalities were practiced by the poor. No sense of social obligation to misfortune was entertained by the well-to-do. An ancient tradition accounted for prosperity as the certified evidence of divine approval. Occasionally some far-seeing prophet had denounced that sophistry, but Dives and his multitude quite outnumbered Amos and his minority; and the fallacy was generally believed. This seriously complicated the problems of life for the poor. They were not only hungry, but forsaken. Were they not bad people, cringing under the frown of Jehovah, they would not be hungry.

Doubtless this explains the very considerable interest

Jesus manifested in the plight of the poor. It was not so much that he wished to see them possessed of more food and better clothing. He was chiefly concerned over their self-conceded inferiority and their depressing sense of being neglected of their God. When he announced, in a little synagogue at the very beginning of his ministry, that he had come to preach good news to the poor, it was his hope that the discoveries he had made of life's real imperatives might transform these beaten, sullen, despairing unfortunates into self-respecting citizens of a spiritual commonwealth, conscious of their equality with the prosperous in the esteem of their common Father.

To the rich he spoke in vigorous terms concerning their social responsibilities; but, while these admonitions were presented to them in the presence of the poor, there is no indication that the latter ever found, in these remarks, any encouragement to rebel against the obvious injustice of their conventionally assigned place in the scheme of things. To the best of our information, there was never so much as a protest raised by the poor against the rich as a result of Jesus' addresses on the subject of social justice.

Nothing is clearer than that the Master expected the poor to find their contentment through their own resources, without banking upon what the rich might do for them if properly motivated by sympathy and a desire to see life's benefits more equitably distributed. In his opinion, the poor would have to be more generous with one another if they hoped to be happy. Happiness always came through giving, rather than getting. That principle applied to the poor as well as to the rich. Poverty had faced life with a whimper. When it extended its hand, it was always with palm up. When the palm is turned up, the corners of the mouth turn down. If the poor were to be happy, they must learn to confer benefits.

The main trouble of the poor was greed. It was even an uglier greed than the greed of the rich, because it dealt with such insignificant things. The greed that leads men of substance to quarrel and cheat and lie over important deals in farms and mines is reprehensible enough, but it is not quite so disgraceful and defiling as a down-on-all-fours squabble in an alley over a crust. Verily, the poor were in a sad plight. Even their iniquities were more disgusting than the same type of iniquities as practiced by the prosperous. Not much wonder if Jesus hoped to be able to bring good news to the poor. They needed it. He never said that they were more worth saving than the wealthy, but he considered their problems entirely different from the problems of the rich. They were threatened with an inferiority complex which increased the hazard of their despair and placed a premium upon their resignation to habitual mendicancy. The only way to lift them out of this low mental state was to put them in the position of donors, rather than beneficiaries. No spiritual progress could be possible to the man who was so intent upon receiving that he had lost all interest in contributing something of himself to the world; and that went for the day laborer just as insistently as for the rich banker.

In various ways, Jesus sets forth this principle, enunciating it in his public addresses and private conversations. The most effective presentation of it occurs in the miracle traditionally known as the multiplication of the loaves and fishes. That this event was considered of vast importance in the opinion of the evangelists is attested by the fact that all four of them record it, with full details—the only miracle reported by the entire group of the gospel writers.

II

Once the public claims a man, he is not permitted the usual privileges of the private citizen. He may not even mourn the loss of a dead friend in the seclusion customarily granted to the less conspicuous. As individuals, the general public may entertain a decent respect for a man's feelings, but the mass mind is singularly lacking in any fineness of sensibility toward the natural emotions of persons prominent in the public eye.

John the Baptist, whom Jesus had declared to be the greatest man of his generation, has just been executed, at the command of Herod Antipas, after two years of solitary confinement in the basement of the gloomy, old castle of Mæcharus, down in the vicinity of the Dead Sea. A few loyal disciples of the fiery prophet, who, since John's incarceration, have been following Jesus in his Galilean ministry, are today returned from a sad errand. They are bowed with grief. The valorous Nazarite had paid the full penalty of his audacity in speaking too candidly before a petty kinglet. His friends have done what little they could, giving the mangled body a decent burial and paying it the tribute of their tears. And now they are back, seeking comfort of the one person in the world who seems to be on good terms with sorrow.

All northern Galilee was, at this hour, in a ferment of excitement over the stirring ministry of Jesus. No longer was there any problem of trying to interest the public in the new gospel. Jesus' only perplexity was the size and temper of the crowds that surged about him at all hours and in all places.

We must not overlook the frequent remark of the gospel narrators in their observation that the people "trod upon one another." This phrase has served only to show us the size of the congregations. We may also interpret it to be indicative of the mood of these congregations. Apparently the people who wanted to hear Jesus wasted very little courtesy on one another. Herein is a strange thing. Had these addresses of Jesus concerned anything else than the things they did concern, it would be easier to understand the rib-digging elbows of the men and women who pushed and shouldered in these crowds. Were Jesus offering counsel on the most effective processes of grabbing benefits out of other people's hands, one could better account for the mood of inquirers who, to be in the front rank, trampled upon their neighbors; but it is a queer sight to see Jesus serenely discoursing of the self-effacing love which makes life worth the living, and the affectionate neighborliness every man must practice who desires to increase his spiritual stature, while his audience is at that moment displaying a spirit of unfriendliness and crude discourtesy.

Of course, we do not charge this to the ineffective-ness of the speaker. It only makes us understand, afresh, the serious need of Jesus' gospel. We see here not a resigned, impotent, inert multitude of rags and tatters strolling with the dragging heels of dull despair into the Master's presence, but a sweating pack of ill-tempered people, jostling one another in their selfish itch to secure good places to see and hear.

If it be thought that this is a strange state of mind for people to be in who are seeking light on the subject of their own spiritual development, we may study the curious psychology of it at closer range by observing the mood of very many persons, today, who apparently seek the gospel in no better temper. Any pastor of a church whose clientele exceeds its seating capacity can testify to the queer manner in which people carry on when, arriving tardily at a Sunday-morning service, they find their favorite pews occupied and must sit elsewhere. Now and again black looks are turned toward the stranger who commits the audacity of sharing the seat of the scornful. On Easter, swarms seek the House of the Lord to hear the tidings of everlasting life, premised upon mutual love and neighborliness, and in too many cases stand scowlingly sullen, if not indeed boisterously aggrieved, because the family pew is filled. On many occasions, in crowded churches, the creed might more appropriately attest its belief in the commotion, rather than the communion, of saints.

Crowds seem to be very much alike in mood, no matter what they have come to see or hear. Jesus' congregations were no more orderly or good-natured than any other crowds, apparently. Let him enter a house, the crowd stuffed itself through the windows and jammed the open doorways. Once it chopped a hole in the roof.

Today, the mourning friends of the late John the Baptist have arrived, and in a few broken words have told their story. It is clear that this day properly belongs to them. Immediately Jesus suggests that they all go away to some secluded spot "and rest awhile." One wishes we had a full report of the consolation the Master offered to these bereaved men as he sat with them in the little sailboat *en route* to the further shore of the Sea of Galilee.

But the curious pack was not to be avoided, even today. A huge multitude scurried after the little company, followed along to the beach, watched the boat put off, noted its course, and resolved to pursue it around the shore road. It may be presumed that not very many in that jostling crowd of five thousand men did not know exactly how wide the Sea of Galilee was at the point where the crossing was being made by that boat. It was easily eight miles. Around the shore road, the obvious destination of the ship was fully twelve miles away. It would be a three-hour trip on foot.

Moreover, it may be presumed that there were not many people in the pursuing crowd who did not know something about the nature of the country on the other side of the lake. It was a sparsely settled region, because the land was sterile. It was a sufficiently unfriendly soil to be called a desert. Let us make sure we have these facts clearly in hand before we set forth in pursuit of that receding sail. Five thousand men, not to speak of many women and children, are starting out on an excursion requiring at least six hours to complete. No one of them knew how long the session would last, over there, but everybody knew it would take six hours to go and return.

An active imagination may conclude that this crowd was probably composed, for the most part, of people who were not in the habit of stopping at inns and taverns for accommodations while tramping to neighboring villages on business errands or visits to friends. Exactly how many of these five thousand men would deliberately set forth on a twenty-four-mile round trip on foot, without a sandwich in their wallets, cannot be guessed. Jesus, whose uncannily accurate estimates of percentages occasionally brings us up with a start of surprise, believed that in any company of people, going out to accomplish something, one-half would be prepared to do everything but the real thing they had gone to do. He pictures a typical situation of the sort in his parable of the ten virgins who went out to meet a wedding party. All ten were in gala attire; all had lamps; all desired to sit later at the banquet. Half of them lacked the oil necessary to furnish the welcome to the wedding procession.

One would imagine that not more than twenty-five hundred men out of five thousand would set out on a six-hour trudge through the sand, with a desert as their destination, without pausing to stuff a biscuit and a smoked eel into their pockets.

III

It was late afternoon in the desert. The sun was low. Nobody had paid attention to the time. The Master had been speaking, and the crowd had welded itself into one solid chunk, hanging on his words. And now the sermon was ended. The disciples are eager to have the people dismissed and sent on their way. They may have felt a sense of responsibility for the welfare of these people. True, the crowd had come here without invitation; but here it was, nevertheless. The disciples' solicitude for the throng does them credit. We must not overlook this item as we pass.

Their suggested solution to the problem, however, shows them to be in the market, themselves, for some more practical counsel on the subject of altruism. The best they can do, in this situation, is to send the people away.

The Master suggests that the people be given their supper before they go. But what an idea! How hopelessly impracticable! Philip makes a hasty computation of the demand and announces that two hundred denarii would not be enough to buy food for so many people, even if each man were given but a morsel. And they did not have two hundred denarii. It is unlikely that they had one hundred, or ten. It was doubtful if that much bread was to be had, in these parts, at any price.

"What have you? Go and see!" This was a significant query and an important command. In response to that query and that command many a man has risen to usefulness and joy from a predicament seemingly hopeless. Upon inquiry, the disciples learn that there is a little boy in the crowd with a lunch basket. He has heard the disciples' announcement that they are looking for food, and has offered his meager supply—five loaves and two fishes. The disciples take the basket and present it to Jesus. They did not entertain any notion that this was an answer to the problem. They brought it up merely as a testimony that there was no food to be had, and this proved it. Here were five thousand men, and five little rolls. Perhaps Jesus would understand, now, how ridiculous it was to let these people stay here any longer in the face of the facts.

According to the story, Jesus bade all the people sit down on the grass in companies of fifties. There was a great feat of altruism about to be performed here, but apparently the mass mind needed to be broken up in the interest of the miracle's success. Fifty constituted about as large a social unit as could be made to serve this peculiar situation. So, somewhat bewildered but obedient, the great multitude resolved itself into fifties, and waited.

We will do well not to miss the practical psychology at work here. Many of us have followed with interest the modern evolution of altruism, from the process by which various groups of philanthropic persons, keenly zealous for the success of special forms of charitable effort, called public attention to the needs of their respective projects, thus putting in the field perhaps so many as twenty "campaigns" annually for funds to support these humanitarian endeavors. In the interest of efficiency there evolved the "Community Chest" which, in a concerted drive for money to carry all these agencies, accomplished the task with apparent success and satisfaction to all parties concerned.

It appears, now, from the experience of most cities, that the unit comprehended by the "Community Chest" is too large. When we had one group working especially for the Day Nursery, another for the Tuberculosis Hospital, another for the Boy Scouts, another for the Maternity Home, etc., each of these companies of zealous people contrived to make its case and secure adequate support. For a few seasons the new idea of a larger unit of endeavor, as comprehended by the "Community Chest," seemed to justify itself. Whether its success was due to the fact that it was operating under a still unspent momentum previously generated by the separate societies, or to the novelty the solicitors found in the new organization, we may not be quite sure. But we are sure that public interest in a pooled effort on the part of a city's philanthropies to secure the necessary funds to operate them all is on the wane.

In our effort to standardize and mechanize every human interest, we are making many of our working units too large to be practical. A typical case in point is the present execution of our prohibition laws. The finest enforcement of the law against the sale of intoxicants was had when the unit was the township. The law was still kept very well, even if not quite so unanimously, when the county became the unit of legislation and enforcement. When the whole state went dry, the unit was larger than it should have been, in most cases, to be satisfactorily effective. When the entire nation went dry, responsibility for the execution of the law seemed to dissolve. Obviously, the unit of legislation and enforcement was too large to conserve the necessary interest of the people in the success of the movement. This is not to discuss the merits of prohibition, as such, but only to consider the psychology involved in the various processes employed to free the land of the abuses invariably attending the liquor traffic.

Jesus seats his five thousand men in companies of fifty. The thing he proposed to do was going to be difficult enough, even with the group method. It would be helpful to this movement if the five thousand could be broken up into something like families of people who would face one another at close range, with a sense of responsibility to see that their group did not show up at a disadvantage in comparison with neighboring groups. Let us give some attention to this lesson who have been bent on mergers and coöperative efforts, on the ground that we could save much "overhead expense" and a deal of reduplicated effort by centralizi'' our organizations. With plenty of object lessons ready taught on this subject, it may not be long befo. we become convinced that the Galilean way of dealing with the public, if it is ever to accomplish anything high and noble, deserves respectful attention.

The people are all seated in companies on the grass, waiting expectantly for some great event. All knew it had to do with their supper. Doubtless there were a large number of people in that multitude who really wished they had the courage to obey the promptings of their own hearts. For an hour they had been listening to a summons to embrace a life program of helpfulness. They had not been promised that their poverty would be relieved, but assured that their contentment could be increased. They had been living selfishly, intent upon getting, rarely projecting their lives in any form of constructive service. There may have been many, many men in that throng of five thousand who, when the disciples were inquiring for food, wished they had the valor to empty their pockets of the little they had brought for their own use. Yesterday they might have dragged out their lunch, unwrapped it, and eaten it in the presence of any number of hungry people, without a detaining thought about the selfishness of the act. Today, after this sermon, it was hard to do it. Each man who had had forethought enough to provide for himself hoped to slip away presently out of the crowd and eat what he had. And now they are all alert to see what will happen.

Jesus calls for silence and announces that he will lead in prayer. He has the little boy's basket in his hands, and gives thanks for this food. How seriously we need to have been informed as to the exact nature of that prayer! What a vast amount of Pauline metaphysics, Johannine visions of eternity, and Petrine counsel on the submissions of one social group to another would we cheerfully exchange for a word-for-word report of that grace which Jesus said, in the desert, over these five little loaves and two fishes.

But, knowing what happened later, our imagination is not heavily taxed to speculate on at least the structural features of that prayer. One may reasonably believe that Jesus gave thanks for the friendliness and graciousness of this little boy who, aware of the sacrifice he was making in offering to divide his supper with such a large multitude of people, most of them strangers to him, nevertheless had presented it to be distributed because he wished to share. One finds it not inconsistent to believe that Jesus thanked God for the happiness that is to be had by sharing; and, on behalf of the lad, offered gratitude for the abiding joy that was now accruing to him through this altruistic act. May he not have prayed, also, that this same happiness, to be had only through neighborliness, might come into many hearts here assembled?

So there was a miracle! The disciples gathered about the Master, the prayer having ended, and stood at attention while he broke the little loaves into tiny bits, preparatory to feeding the vast throng. The waiting people realized, now, what was about to happen. I think the fifties must have begun to respond to the irresistible urge about the time Jesus was seen breaking the little loaves into crumbs. I do not see how they could have borne much more of this without taking some action. All that was required, in each company, was for some one man—a little more alert than his neighbors—to put a hand into his wallet and draw out, and pass to the man seated at his side, with the request that he have some.

The disciples are now passing through the ranks,

distributing the morsels of bread and fish. Everybody is getting enough to eat. Everybody is having a good time. The little boy who gave up his basket has both cheeks and both hands full. It was, indeed, a miraculous feast; for nothing short of a miracle of divine grace could have softened the mass heart of a multitude so discourteous and greedy as this particular throng that had no respect for the bereaved disciples' grief, and so little regard for one another that they pushed and trampled in an effort to advantage themselves.

By this miracle of altruism, they were all fed. No one was left hungry. Indeed, it was found that they had more food than could be eaten, and twelve baskets of broken fragments were collected. We are not told where these baskets came from, or how they arrived on the ground, but we are entitled to think as we please about that. All who wish to believe that certain persons, in this multitude, came over here into the desert with empty baskets, expecting to gather something to take home with them, are hereby granted full rights to extract from that theory whatever helpful lesson seems to be indicated.

IV

Let us, for just a moment, consider the story exactly as it stands in the text, completely neglecting to listen for the "overtones" in this symphony of love in action.

The people are all hungry—five thousand and more of them. They had left their homes in the forenoon, had trudged twelve miles through the heat, had listened to an address; and now they are hungry. Not a man of them has had the good judgment to bring a lunch along. Nobody in this whole two acres of hungry people has brought food but one small boy. He now offers his basket. Jesus gives thanks and breaks the loaves and fishes. The disciples distribute the feast to the multitude. The bread grows in their hands. The people eat. They are amazed. The more they eat, the more they have left! This is magical food! It is a wonder they can eat it at all. One would think their bewilderment would deaden their appetites. But they eat this miraculous food until they are all satisfied. A great miracle has been wrought. *What* miracle? Let somebody, who prefers this interpretation of the story, kindly step forth and say just what is the lesson taught here!

Something has happened that never happened before? Well, what is the good of that, if the case rests there? Something has happened here that will never happen again? Obviously, that is bad. Is it so important this multitude shall not miss a meal that we must have Heaven importuned for power to feed five thousand with five biscuits? Did Jesus operate his own life on the theory that a man must on no account miss a meal? Did he ever indicate that bread was of such concern to men's lives that one was justified in employing divine power to create it? What is the exact difference, after all, between the wrongness of turning stones into bread in the Jeshimon Wilderness, and turning five little loaves into a feast for five thousand in the Peræan Desert?

Now that the magical feast is over and the twelve baskets of fragments are collected, what high purpose has been served? Are these five thousand any better off than they were before? Stuffed with bread and fish —granted. But shall we be content with that as the total result of this miracle? They are astonished over it all. But are they any better off for being astonished? Did the Son of Man come to bewilder and befuddle, or to seek and to save, that which was lost? It is high time we satisfied ourselves on this point, if we wish to find helpfulness in these stories of Christ's divine power to make human life more worthy of our Father's regard.

The people are all going home now. They have been well fed and well puzzled. They had gone out bearing a host of serious problems, their minds disheveled with mystifying questions about life, and are now going home with all the queries they had, to the total of which has been added yet one more. Something has happened today that had never happened before and is never to happen again. They have been to a show. A great magician has performed for them. The exhibition has cost them nothing, and, because they do not understand how it was accomplished, they have learned nothing. Add up all the assets accruing to them, draw a line, and compute the total result of this spectacular event in terms of its benefits to this particular company of people or to the world at large. After all is said for it, what was achieved?

Interpreted as a miraculous division of food, rather than as a miraculous multiplication of food, this event instantly rises to a position of high idealism. We have here a really remarkable story of Jesus' compassionate and helpful interest in the welfare of needy people. He knows and teaches that happiness arrives through mutual service; that it is more blessed to give than to receive; that unless joy be shared, it perishes. He effects a practical demonstration of this fact to a great company of greedy, selfish, discourteous people. It is a miracle. And the most interesting feature of it is that the miracle has been repeated, and is being repeated, every day. By the grace of Christ's enduring influence so much progress has been made in practical altruism that today it would be considered a very ordinary and natural event for a large crowd of people to share with one another whatever they had in some emergency. In the Peræan Desert it takes a miracle to make people sensible of their obligations to others less fortunate than themselves. That event occurred when the Golden Rule was taking its first steps. It was in the days when Jesus defined neighborliness by telling the story of the Good Samaritan who was so magnanimous that he picked up a wounded stranger along the roadside and ministered to his needs, after representatives of two religions had passed by, indifferent to this case of distress. We have lived to see the Golden Rule functioning so well that the Good Samaritan type is in the majority. It is now no great credit to a man that he should pick up a wounded stranger, even at some risk to himself: it would be a public shame to him if he did not.

"Greater works than these!" Jesus hoped that we would take these high principles which he taught and make them universally effective. If he ever accomplished any great feat by faith which is impossible for us to achieve by faith, why did he ask us to follow him and strive to be like him? Whatever may be the minor differences in our beliefs about Jesus, let us all try to follow him. But to venture hopefully upon that path we must believe that he *can* be followed.

CHAPTER EIGHT

THE HIGHER HEREDITY

I

IT WAS observed in a preceding chapter that the latest of the gospels differs from the writings of the synoptists in the important particular that this document evidently aims at presenting a series of impressionistic portraits symbolizing the generic facts at issue in Jesus' teachings.

So essential is it that we have an understanding of this motive and an appreciation of this method as employed by the author of the Fourth Gospel, one has grounds for believing that the book merely muddles our thinking about Jesus' ministry unless we approach this mysterious writing with these facts well in hand.

We have come now to the investigation of a miracle —reported only in this gospel—alleged to have been performed upon a man blind from his birth. The narrative is so crowded with incident that it is as a picture in which several exposures seem to have been made on one plate. Obviously it is a synthetic portrait.

Perhaps this point may be fairly well illustrated by reference to some of the most celebrated masterpieces of sacred art, in which various more or less irrelevant events of the Master's life are synthetized on one canvas, with a major issue predominating, and other loosely related episodes employed to provide "atmosphere."

There seems no need to multiply cases of this well-known style of artistic treatment. One instance will suffice. In Raphael's "Transfiguration," frequently conceded to be the greatest work of the most gifted painter who ever dealt with these high themes, Jesus is seen floating in a lambent cloud above the truncated summit of the mountain, attended by the glorified spirits of Moses and Elijah in flowing robes. Prone upon the ground, directly below them, are the figures of Peter, James, and John, posed in attitudes of awe and bewilderment. Only a few feet beneath the mountain's summit, where this pageant is occurring, the nine disciples are endeavoring unsuccessfully to cure a lad's epilepsy. The dominant figure among the nine is pointing toward the radiant figure of the Saviour in the cloud, presumably admonishing the sick boy to seek strength from that source. The Scriptures do not bear Raphael out in this; but the artist is unquestionably justified in the obvious lesson implied by his treatment of the subject. On the ground, near by the pointing disciple, sits a dissatisfied scholar with an open book in which he is finding something contrary to the procedure of the disciples. Over the shoulder of this ten-foot mountain a village may be seen, and beyond the village the sea.

To include all this on one meager canvas, Raphael

found it necessary to make his mountain a mere knoll, thus sacrificing actual truth in the cause of impressionism. One does not cavil at the treatment. Persons who would criticize this painting on the ground of its obvious inconsistencies should restrict their judgment of artistic matters to the field of photography, and omit impressionistic art from their program altogether.

Again, in the Church of the Holy Sepulchre in Jerusalem the tourist finds in close proximity historic shrines fixing the sites of strategic incidents in the Master's career which could be included under one roof only by the exercise of an imagination wholly unconcerned about facts, figures, and accuracies.

The Gospel according to St. John is a group of word portraits. Into each of these pictures there is crowded a vast amount of incidental materials. The student is not to conclude that the minor issues which serve "atmospherically" in these impressionistic sketches are of negligible importance, in and of themselves, but relatively unimportant in any other settings than those which give each of them the full right of way. It is necessary, therefore, to a proper study of these pictures in the Fourth Gospel, that we painstakingly analyze all the incidents included in a single narrative, giving each detail as much room as it obviously appears to deserve in that particular situation, but refusing to be distracted, by these minor issues, from the main consideration.

In the story now before us the day is the Sabbath,

and the bulk of the controversy among the persons interested in the miracle centers in the perennial problem of Sabbath observance. It is to be remembered that Jesus received much criticism from the ultra-conservatives because of his belief and practice of the principle that the Sabbath was made for man, and not man for the Sabbath. The author of the Fourth Gospel is quite insistent that this criticism should be amply recorded. We find this fact recurring frequently in this document. But let us make sure we do not permit this episodal matter to loom up so large as to obscure the real point at issue, which was something other than a debate over what a man might lawfully do on the seventh day of the week.

In the course of the story the parents of the erstwhile blind man are importuned by the critics to state their own estimate of Jesus' ability to exercise divine power. These aged people are aware that to admit belief in the Galilean's capacity as a healer will amount to apostasy from their religious faith. They will be put out of the synagogue and suffer the ostracism which excommunication involved. Here again the author of the Fourth Gospel is revealing the mood and temper of the forces hostile to Jesus. He is picturing a typical situation which might easily occur in the experience of persons manifesting an active interest in the new Galilean gospel. Let us not permit this feature of the picture to absorb too much of our attention. Granting it to be important as a separate fact, we must make sure it does not get completely out of drawing until it takes up all the room. Just as in Raphael's "Transfiguration," the carping Pharisee with the open book is a figure five times the dimension of the enhaloed Lord, so, in John's portrait of the miracle we are to study, the hostility of the critics, the cowardice of the parents, and the general clamor of the contentious brawlers in their quarrel over Jesus' right to exercise divine power are apt to clutter the mind of the student to such extent that he misses the main point.

Having then reduced all the incidental details of this story to what seems to be their respective values, we face two essential considerations, to wit: *It is unimportant that we should locate the blame for human misfortunes;* and *it is entirely possible for Christian idealism to overcome hereditary infirmities.*

II

This ninth chapter of the Fourth Gospel is one of the noisiest in the book. People are gesticulating frantically, shouting impertinent questions, and hurling maledictions at one another. It is difficult to think clearly in the midst of this confusion. But, however tempestuous the scene becomes, let us keep it in mind that the entire event begins with and centers in the query of the disciples as they pass a man who is known by them to have been blind from his birth, "Whose fault was it that this man was born blind?" Now this is the exact motion before the house, and we will do well to dissect it carefully out of all the general tangle of incidents included in the story, and appraise it on its own merits.

To quote the record literally, the disciples wish to know whether this man's congenital blindness was his parents' fault or his own. It would appear that the second phase of the query quite sufficiently answers itself. A man blind from his birth could hardly be held accountable for his affliction. We may omit that part of the question from consideration, seeing it has no meaning whatsoever. If interested to know why it appears here at all, one may find some explanation in the fact that the typical query of the period invariably offered an alternative. Every dilemma, among these people, had two horns. What the disciples really want to know is, Where is the blame to be located for this man's blindness?

Here is a question which explains a vast amount of human wretchedness. There is a type of mind quite obsessed with the idea that it is important to fix the blame for all of our difficulties. The victim of this psychosis locates an adequate cause for every misfortune, and then proceeds to magnify and illuminate that alleged cause until it drives all other considerations into complete eclipse.

For example: a man has lost his money through a bad investment. He had lived economically, saved against a day of need, placed it in unscrupulous hands, and now it is gone. Had there been a suspicion in his mind that the gold mine in which he was invited to invest was located on the thirty-first floor of an office building in some busy metropolis, he would have been warranted in making an investigation of that enterprise to discover whether the money he was lending it would go toward the operation of mining machinery or an expensive limousine and a roulette wheel.

Now that the blow has fallen, however, and the money is irretrievably lost, the unfortunate investor may properly conclude that he has already spent enough in that quarter, without putting in the balance of his life secreting poisonous hate from every gland and spilling bitterness over everything he touches. He has paid enough. Why more? What possible good can accrue to him now by ruminating upon his injury and despising the institution that has defrauded him? All he gets out of it is the development of an unpleasant psychosis that decreases his vitality, spoils his appetite, robs him of sleep, and sours his life to the extent of making him disagreeable in his own house and a nuisance at his club.

Who cares—now that it is all done—exactly where the blame should rest? Let the injured person locate that blame if he likes, and fill the rest of his days with scorn for the malefactor—what does he get beyond a lowered resistance to diseases and an ache that grows bigger as it grows older? By some process he must subordinate that obsession or it will do him up. How shall he subordinate it? That is the question involved in this ninth chapter of John.

Let us consider another hypothetical case of "blame fixing." This is a very important matter and we can afford to give it the attention it deserves. If little Susie has developed symptoms of scarlet fever, any noisy hysterics about the "criminal carelessness of that awful woman on the street car with the sick baby" will neither reduce Susie's temperature nor increase the effectiveness of Susie's mother as she now confronts her new responsibilities.

"I just knew it, at the time! I was certain that wretched child had some contagious disease!" moans Susie's mother, in the arms of Susie's nurse, who at that moment should have been left free to look out for Susie's welfare. "That cruel, heartless, stupid woman, going about spreading this horrible affliction!"

Well, if that is the way Susie came by her scarlet fever, then that is probably how she got it. But however she may have come by it, she has it. She must be cured of it, if possible. Her recovery may depend considerably upon good nursing, which she may be able to have if nobody in the family persists in keeping the whole place in an uproar.

Even if it could be proved, beyond the shadow of a reasonable doubt, that the awful woman in the street car had known her baby had scarlet fever and was carrying it about for the malicious purpose of spreading the disease, and was arrested, sentenced to life imprisonment, or hanged by the neck until dead, little Susie would still have the scarlet fever, her recovery depending, exactly as it would depend if the cause of the trouble were unknown, upon good nursing, which Susie cannot have unless the racket is reduced at her home.

If the house is on fire, any frantic lamentations over the alleged incompetency of the electrician who bungled the job of wiring the attic accomplish nothing but that much more excitement added to the general din. The problem just now is that the house is on fire, and it is highly desirable that the fire be put out before it does any more damage than it has already done. There is no other problem, at the moment, but this one: we must put out the fire, if possible. If we cannot, then it may be assumed that the house burns down and we must either find another house or live out of doors. But as to who may be responsible for the fire, how far he may be culpable, what punishment he deserves, what remorse he ought to experience—these matters only clutter the problem and make clear thinking and effective action difficult.

If the best-loved member of the household is dead, all the bitter reproaches uttered concerning the physician's incompetency are in vain. All that is left now of our loved one is the memory of the love we gave and the love that was requited to us. Love becomes exceptionally valuable when fixed in a solution of tears; but if the tincture of bitterness be poured in, it is spoiled by that much. There may have been a time when the skill and zeal of the attending physician might well have been inquired into. That time is past. Of course, in the stress of unprepared-for anguish, the bereaved may be pardoned many frantic words; and if he wishes to talk like a fool while under the stunning impact of the blow, there will be none to censure him. But even his most understanding friends have a right to hope that he will eventually pull himself together and behave like a sane man.

Sometimes the blame fixer's assault turns toward the skies. It is all God's fault. Not very much had this man thought about God before; but now he thinks about Him a great deal, and not very pleasantly. He is now able to recognize, for the first time, the divine hand; had never seen it before; knows nothing about it as an open, friendly, helpful hand. His first sight of it is a clenched fist! He is not being led by the hand of God: he is being menaced by the fist of God!

He becomes quite adept in defining his philosophy. God had singled out this household to be used as clinical material in His experimental laboratory for testing the effect of certain vicissitudes upon the human soul. He had marked these people from infancy, bringing them up for the exclusive purpose of seeing how much they could stand; and now, having demonstrated that they cannot stand any more, He decides they are unfit to survive their vivisection, so He is going to finish them. A hard taskmaster—sitting there in heaven on a golden throne, watching His creatures stagger under their pains and burdens; never saying a word, but just sitting there watching, like a cruel boy studying the convulsions of a bug impaled on a pin!

One's friends overlook all this sort of chatter for a little while; but soon the lugubrious whine becomes quite tiresome. A strange whimsy usually disclosed by the "God-scolder" is his belief that he is pious. He does not permit anyone else to speak uncordially about Deity in his presence, reserving that privilege for his own use. He thinks because he takes so great an interest in his relation to God, and speaks so frequently of Him, he must be a very good man. Were he to go about cursing like a drunken pirate, and reviling God in all the lingo known to profanity, he would be lily white in his innocence of sacrilege as compared with the effect of his bitter whimper that God had planned to mistreat him.

Never mind the blame! Here we are, creatures of a day, serving we know not what high purpose, but assured that it must be a very high purpose, or there would not be such a tremendous volume of sacrifice and grief and struggle involved in its evolution. One man may think he has more than his rightful quota of trouble. A pious friend may console him with the thought that perhaps his burdens are heavy because he can bear more than his neighbors. One doubts if there is any evidence to justify such opinion. One wishes there was something to it; but there are no facts to be had sufficient to make a case. One sees people crushed under loads who could not stagger under half that much disaster, and other people, apparently capable of enduring considerable strain, moving jauntily along through life as if insured against heartache. One of the functions of our faith is to accept this matter exactly as it stands, and make no attempt to explain it to ourselves or other people. If everything in life was mathematically distributed, so much load for so much lift, so much grief for so much grit, so much tempest for so much tranquillity, every man taxed just what he can pay, and no more—this would be a vastly different world.

Many persons have notions that they might reorganize things on the basis of a better justice. Omar Khayyám wished he might shatter the scheme to bits and remold it nearer to his heart's desire. If anybody has a technique for doing this, he will find plenty of people interested in his experiment—people who could not very easily be worse off and might welcome any changes. But if no one is prepared to offer a better world or another plan for human existence, it may be presumed that our best happiness lies in accepting this world and this plan with a minimum of complaint. We must stop speculating on how we might carry on if this were another sort of a world and we were somebody else.

"Master, did this man's parents sin, that he was born blind?" Here comes the old query. Now we are going to find out whether God has arranged to penalize a child for the iniquities of his parents. This is a live question. It was never more alive than at this moment. Modern biology has pointed out that all living things carry two sets of chromosomes in every cell of their bodies, said chromosomes derived from their parents, who had received them from their parents. In every drop of blood, in every corpuscle of every tissue, here are these ancestral chromosomes inexorably determining all the motivation and functioning of the legatee.

The only trouble with this theory resides at the point of its forgetting that there are other forces at work in human nature, perhaps not quite so clearly defined as this biological urge which permits examination under a microscope, but no less real because not so cordial toward laboratory inquisitiveness. Whatever may be our theories about hereditary tendencies, we know that natural inclinations, derived from parental sources, can be and are overcome. If, by some definite process of counteracting heredity, our primitive barbarities had not been overcome, we would all be living in tree tops, quarreling over our cocoanuts. Let biology bow down before its precious chromosomes and do all the genuflections required of it by the new scientific ritual which makes men as dogmatic in their chemistry as ever fanatical mystic was in his creed; the fact remains that heredity is worth just what it will fetch, from generation to generation, in a market where ideals have the last word in fixing its value and defining the extent of its authority.

All the great religions have interesting stories to tell about the re-creation possible in men's lives. Paul did not exaggerate when he declared that the Christ-controlled man became a new creature, from whom the old interests had passed away and for whom all things had become new. The nature and extent of the re-creation of a man, wrought through a religion, depends, of course, upon the essential aims of that particular religious philosophy. Buddhism might consider it vastly more important that the seeker be calmed of his mental fevers and disciplined in a steady tranquillity than that he should be propelled into altruistic endeavor or a concern for the happiness of his neighbors. But even a slight reshaping of human motives is so very much preferable to no reshaping at all, that Buddha is entitled to all the praise and honor he can collect from his devotees. Indeed, their very act of gratitude for the gift of soul calmness makes them more capable of achieving it.

It is a mistake to conclude that Christianity alone has the capacity to offset and counteract unfortunate hereditary tendencies. Not infrequently, the new motive which re-creates a man is the acquisition of love for some other person. Many a man has been completely made over—at least to all outward seeming—by the influence of a woman to whom he has given his heart. Under the magic of her wishes, he grows to like and enjoy things he had previously detested and to lose interest in things he had previously considered essential to his happiness.

Sometimes personal ambition will step in and re-create a character. There are many things the man would do which he discovers are not expedient if he proposes to succeed in his business or profession; and because his ambition to succeed is of greater concern than the gratification of his other wishes, he sublimates his desires until, at length, he completely loses interest in everything that menaces the satisfaction of his dominant desire. Biology to the contrary, human character may be changed whenever an ideal is accepted which proves strong enough to overcome all the hereditary tendencies operating to that ideal's disadvantage.

The history of Christian civilization, as compared with all other civilizations, indicates that the most impelling motive known to humanity is the ideal comprehended in Jesus' establishment of men's common brotherhood premised upon God's universal Fatherhood. He taught that men should treat one another as brothers because that was their exact relationship. They were all sons of one spiritual Father. Here was an hereditary urge that took precedence over any and all other tendencies. Let the chromosomes take note, and govern themselves accordingly: we are the sons of God: it doth not yet appear what we may become, but we know that when God shall have been made clearly

manifest to us, we shall be found to be like Him.   This
is the fundamental thesis of the Christ teaching.

III

In the light of the foregoing, how natural it was
that Jesus should assert the power of his discovery
about life's organization on a basis of God's Fatherhood
and men's brotherhood as entirely competent to deal
with all of humanity's problems.   Here, for example,
was a man born in darkness.   Jesus had come to bring
light.   He had come to offer a new vision that would
permit men to see beauties and glories in a world
where God's Fatherhood prevailed over every other
fact.

Pursuant to his promise that this new consciousness,
arriving in the experience of a man, would re-create
him, unbind him, and make him supreme over his difficulties, Jesus does something to this blind man that lifts
him into an ecstasy of joy.   When it was all over, and
the contention incident to the miracle had spent its
fury, "some of the Pharisees which were with him said
unto him, 'Are we blind, also?' "

It is entirely natural, of course, that the minstrel
who provides us with this epic should fill his poem with
enough properties to make it histrionically appealing.
The purpose of our present treatment of the miracle is
not to destroy the conventional interpretation of it,
but to look for the "overtones."   Obviously, the lesson

which stands permanently accessible here, to all who seek a better understanding of our human miseries, is the fact that Christ brings a new light that permits men to see, who previously were blind. Even the Pharisees, assured as they were of the lucidity of their vision, become distrustful of their complacency and, in the face of this poor man's new ecstasy, exclaim, "Are we blind, also?"

One wonders whether there is much to be gained by a critical review of the minor incidents in this story; for doubtless all persons who wish to interpret this miracle as a gift of spiritual understanding, vouchsafed by "the light of the world," will be content to rest the case there; and all persons who insist upon the literal acceptance of the spittle, the clay, and the therapeutic waters of Siloam, will not be satisfied with our interpretation, anyway. But, in fairness to everybody, let us take a look at the text and deduce what we may from it.

Jesus has just said, "As long as I am in the world, I am the light of the world."

Now the world is a very large institution. Whoever would make free use of any comment about "the world" ought to understand that he is talking about something of vast extent. Jesus, knowing how great the world is, declares that so long as his spirit is in it, he will be its light. He assures men that if they accept this light, they can see. Here is a divine ideal phrased in the most lofty terms. We dislike to be plunged into the next sentence, for it seems to be pitched in a totally different key. "When he had thus spoken, he spat on the ground, and made clay of the spittle, and anointed the eyes of the blind man with the clay; and said to him, 'Go, wash in the pool of Siloam.' "

The conservative—(bless his heart for wanting to accept every word of this pictorial narrative; for it does a man credit to make full use of all the data he can get concerning Jesus' deeds)—really ought to be told that saliva was thought, in ancient times, to have a remarkable value in curing cases of blindness. Whether it had any healing virtue or not is no affair of ours. The fact remains that it was so considered. The Emperor Vespasian is said to have restored sight to a blind man by spitting in his eyes, and Æsculapius employed this technique in his medical practice. Certain clays were alleged to have therapeutic virtues. Everybody knew of the beneficial qualities of the water in the Pool of Siloam; people were to be seen about it at all hours, availing themselves of its healing powers.

So, that being true, "the light of the world" spits upon the ground, compounds a paste of clay, and orders the blind man to the Pool of Siloam. Indeed, it reads as if the narrator was doing two separate stories here —one on top of the other—in the same chronicle. The story, on its high plane, concerns a "light of the world," an ecstasy of bliss on the part of the restored patient as he comes into the possession of his new spiritual vision, and the anxiety of thoughtful bystanders lest they, themselves, were not seeing quite so well as they might. The story, in its more materialistic aspect, deals with all the known techniques for the relief of blindness, as if the author were eager to make the miracle sound as convincing as possible. It is as if he, in composing it, had doubted the capacity of many persons (as well he might) to consider an act motivated by divine power unless there was a physical wonder wrought, and at the last minute had decided that the cure would be all the sounder for a few medicines. We must handle this situation with becoming reverence; but does it not rasp the sensibilities just a little to see one who has just affirmed that he is "the light of the world," stirring his saliva in the dust as a prefatory gesture to offering a man the sublime gift of an ennobling vision?

Blindness was and is common in that backward land where too much bigotry of opinion has always prevailed to permit the free course of new discoveries in the field of therapeutics. There were many blind men on the streets—blind from their birth. According to the literal story, Jesus restores sight to one of them. He does not say how he has done it. People can draw their own conclusions. All who think that the clay was the thing that proved beneficial can now renew their experiments with clay. Those who think there is any virtue in saliva can put more saliva on their sightless eyes. The Pool of Siloam will be visited by more unfortunates than ever before. There has been a terrific hubbub about this miracle in the city, and everybody is talking about it. All the blind men are excited. It is pitiful to see them clawing about in the dust where Jesus had stood, hoping to happen upon some of this magic clay that had been vitalized by the spittle of the light of the world. It is equally pitiful to see them tapping the pavement on their way to the Pool of Siloam. For, do what they will, this miracle was only a little demonstration of what divine power could do if it had a notion to help men out of their blindness. One sees them kneeling on the flagging, about the Pool of Siloam, dipping up water and weeping bitter tears.

All things considered, it seems better to let Jesus be the light of the world, as he said, than a quack doctor whose encouragement of ignorant people's superstitions only leads them into fresh disappointments. There was a miracle wrought that day. A man had come by his sight who had always been blind. They asked him how it happened that he now could see, and he replied that he did not know. He dismissed all their queries as of no importance to him. Only one thing was he sure of: "Whereas I was blind, now I see."

The officials put him out of the synagogue. But that was not because Jesus had entered into competition with the synagogue in the business of curing men of blindness. The synagogue made no pretense to cure blindness. The synagogue was devised to offer men new light concerning their relation to God and one another.

Jesus had offered this man something that showed up the synagogue at a decided disadvantage. The Pharisees put the man out. He was finding new life and hope in something they knew he had not discovered under that roof. He saw something they knew they could not see, and as they bolted the doors against him they said, "Are we also blind?"

CHAPTER NINE

A PENTAGONAL PAVILION

I

IT IS Sabbath morning. One of the major festivals of the Jews is on and Jerusalem is crowded. Jesus strolls down to the old Sheep Gate. Around a pool, traditionally believed to be occasionally invested with magical properties of healing, a convention of misery is in session. All sorts of unfortunates are there—blind, lame, palsied.

The Master questions one of these wretched people. The man has been sick for thirty-eight years. Would he like to be made well? He would. Jesus tells him to arise, take up his pallet, and go. He obeys. And Jesus saunters out of the pitiable throng of desperately needy men and women without so much as a backward glance at them.

Do you like this story, as much as you have heard of it? Neither do I.

Perhaps we would better look into the case and see if we have not taken snap judgment. There may be some circumstances here which have not been properly explained to us. It is a pity to let the matter stand this way if it might be cleared up, for we do not want

Jesus presented in this rôle. We have learned to think of him as the most compassionate, merciful, and comradely man who ever lived, and we must not permit that impression to be disturbed. We know exactly how Jesus feels toward people who are in trouble. He wants us to feel the same way. He has some strong words about the callous selfishness of the priest and Levite who, seeing a wounded man along the roadside, passed by with utter indifference to his sorry plight. Surely there is an explanation to be had for this distressing incident at the Pool of Bethesda. Let us see what can be done about it.

The hidden meaning of the miracle which Jesus performed that Sabbath morning is not to be had at the price of a hasty reading. Indeed, it is not to be had at any price, unless it be painstakingly studied with a clear knowledge of the mystic's mood who wrote it. Review it every day, if you like, for a whole lifetime: you will never know what it is about until you acquaint yourself with the rhetorical style and mental habits of its author.

Modern scholarship is not unanimously agreed on the name of the man who wrote the Fourth Gospel. Nobody, at the present hour, is in a position to settle that question. It was quite generally believed, for a little matter of about seventeen hundred and fifty years subsequent to its issue and previous to the dispute about its authorship, that the book was written by "the beloved disciple," John. One man's guess being nearly as good as another's in the absence of reliable authority, let us guess that John wrote it. We have a lot of good reasons for thinking it to be true, though this is no place to canvas them: it would take too long. We will just assume that John wrote the Fourth Gospel. That makes the book very much easier to understand; for if the same man wrote the Gospel according to John and the Revelation of John, we are that much ahead in our endeavor to find out what the Fourth Gospel is driving at, and the reason for the strange processes employed.

After one has wandered, breathless and bewildered, through the ornate and labyrinthine galleries of the Bible's closing pages, completely puzzled over the meanings of its intricately sculptured friezes, the occult legends of its elaborate frescoes, and the baffling ciphers, tokens, and symbolisms of its cabalistic architecture, definitely assured that every tiny sliver of every mosaic on the walls, every device wrought into the pavement, and every character moving in the vast pageants so adroitly staged, is loaded with emblematic significance, one becomes convinced that the man who put up that superb dream edifice possessed an imagination which would have great difficulty in expressing itself on high themes except by the allegorical method.

Let us not be deceived by the apparent simplicity of the Fourth Gospel. Nothing that John would write could be considered simple. Anything that he wrote would be full of pictures. Every picture would brim to its very frame with symbols. This would stand for that, and that would stand for something else. Nor is John very particular about explaining what everything means. Perhaps he assumed that the reader would know what he meant. If so, he assumed too much. The reader does not always or often know. He puts his own imagination to work on these cryptic statements, and deduces whatever sounds most reasonable. Or perhaps he deduces what will most nicely confirm some opinion he holds—some opinion greatly in need of whatever confirmatory props it can put a hand on. (Such opinions should be regarded with suspicion.)

The Revelation of John has sent a lot of fine people to the madhouse; and the fact that many whom it sent failed to arrive and are still at large does not mean that they shouldn't be there, but only that they missed connections.

Few people pause to reflect that the same fancy which evolved the terrific picture book known as The Apocalypse also wrought the Fourth Gospel. We agreed earlier that the Gospel according to John must be viewed in a mood peculiar to this document. It is not the same kind of a writing as the synoptic books. We must reiterate this fact. We must quite insist upon it, this time. The story we are now to examine is perhaps the most cryptic of them all. It presents serious difficulties and demands patient study.

II

Usually, when the story of this miracle wrought at the Pool of Bethesda is read, the mere surface of the text is lightly skimmed. The properties of the little drama are very simple. The case seems clear. If you believe in miracles, you accept it at face value. If you don't believe in miracles, you doubt its truth. Not many listen for the "overtones" in this bit of minstrelsy. But the "overtones" are there, nevertheless.

The event, as recorded in the book, may be briefly sketched as follows:

Upon the flagging, under a sheltering roof, a multitude of miserable people lie waiting the occasional visit of an angel who, according to a common belief of the day, touches the waters of the sacred pool around which they are clustered. It is thought that whoever first enters the pool immediately after the magic is wrought by the angel will be cured of what ails him.

It is to be observed that the most recent translations omit this passage about the angel's visits to the pool. One suspects that the deletion of this sentence was in the interest of making the episode sound more reasonable. If so, the translator's intention is commendable, for the story about the angel is a bit thick and people should not be asked to believe it. Nevertheless, this statement of John's about the angel who occasionally "troubled the waters" was part of his story, and we are not going to make the situation any clearer by refusing to include this feature of it. Indeed, we will find, before we are through with it, that we need the angel to help straighten things out.

On occasion, then, an angel visited the pool. What a great scramble must have ensued among the cripples! The spirit of competition adds excitement to the moment, but what a pitiable state of affairs; for, obviously, the man who was in most serious need of the miraculous bath was the least likely to have it. Somebody else always won the race.

Here lay a helpless invalid, that Sabbath day, still willing to wait and hope. Perhaps some one might happen along at exactly the right moment and help him down into the water. The chances of that were not very good. Passers-by did not seem disposed to take an interest in his predicament, and even with prompt assistance he had no assurance that he would be able to plunge in soon enough to benefit by this magic.

Jesus stops here and surveys the throng of needy people. He falls into conversation with this particular invalid; learns he had been ill for a very long time; inquires if he would like to be cured. The man tells Jesus all about his case. There was nobody to help him. Every time he tried to step down into the water, another was there ahead of him. Jesus offers him instant release from his affliction. The man takes up his little mattress and leaves. Jesus disappears in the gathering throng.

Naturally, our first impression of the story is not satisfactory. We do not like it. At the outset, we find the tale about the angel quite difficult. This was a poor way for an angel to act. Nothing could have been less fair than this heavenly aid offered at the Pool of Bethesda. A common lottery, in which hundreds of gamblers buy tickets, fully aware that only one man can get a prize, is a praiseworthy affair in comparison with this sad business down by the Sheep Gate where a miscellaneous aggregation of unfortunate people sit waiting, day after day, for the angel of the Lord to bless the water. Picture it, if you can. There is a ripple on the pool. A fearful chorus of shrieks breaks loose, pitched in the agonizing treble of desperation. All the poor wretches squirm and wriggle and dig their elbows into the pavement, clawing for a chance to get down there where that ripple appeared. One succeeds. All the rest fail. One is cured; the others stay sick. They sink back, moaning. Some mumble their disappointment; some weep softly into the crooks of their ragged sleeves. Like the idea? Of course, not! What a thoroughly reprehensible angel. If this celestial visitant has any power at all, he has power to cure all these people. He is not a mere specialist, dealing with diseases of the blood and skin; or eye, ear, nose and throat; or cerebral lesions. He touches the water, and whoever jumps in is cured of whatever disease he had. Just one patient, however. The rest can wait until some other day. What an angel! No wonder the recent texts have ruled him out. We should be glad enough, however, that we still have access to the original; for we do most seriously need that angel if we are ever to understand this story.

Be careful that you do not let this angel disappear from the picture. You may be disposed to shout, "Nonsense!" But don't be hasty. There is no nonsense in this story. Hang on to every scrap of it. Not a word dare be missing from it when we study its symbolic significance.

Moving on, now, we find Jesus presented in a manner that does him small credit. He is down there to investigate conditions at the Pool of Bethesda. He knows what an unconscionable fraud the institution is. The reason he takes pity on the man who has tried so long and unsuccessfully to get into the water is because the situation is so manifestly unjust. Anybody could see what a travesty on mercy was being enacted here. Jesus sympathizes with the plight of this discouraged suppliant for healing. He cures him; sends him away hilarious, so hilarious that he forgets he is breaking the law by carrying his mattress on the Sabbath day.

And then Jesus strolls away. Look at this, will you? Jesus divinely intervenes, and cures a man because the arrangements at the Pool of Bethesda were so unfair that only one sufferer could be helped during the season of the angel's visit. Apparently he took but little stock in the ministrations of this mythical winged jester who ran the grim and grisly game near the Sheep Gate. But how much fairer were the arrangements, now that Jesus had taken an interest in its problems? The angel was good for only one patient per season. How much better is the Master's record? Does the story please you? It does not.

With but a little more effort, Jesus can go about among these weeping and groaning wretches and send the poor things away happy. Why, a man who would walk into a situation like that, with all the power of heaven back of him, aware of his ability to release a multitude of people from their miseries and tell them to go home well and strong, and perform a miracle on just one of them and then walk away, serenely indifferent to the outcries of the others—what a deal of explaining he would have to do before anybody could understand how he was the Saviour of the World! So, we do not like the idea. We decide that the whole story must be an elaborate picture of something. John was a great man for pictures. Perhaps he is just letting himself go, here, on a bit of rather difficult symbolism.

III

Back to the beginning, then, for a fresh start. Let us not miss a single detail that might afford a clue. No matter how insignificant a word or phrase may seem, let us turn the light on it.

"There was a feast of the Jews, and Jesus went up

to Jerusalem." The older versions say *"the* feast." That would be the annual Passover affair. It would be intensely interesting if we had something concerning Jesus' thoughts as he walked about the old city on the occasions of these major events of his nation's established religion. The Passover had evolved into a combination State Fair, family reunion, holiday week, and general round-up of social and commercial interests. The great festival had originated as a commemoration of the night when the Hebrews had fled Egypt under the leadership of Moses. Gradually it had become barnacled with all manner of curious accretions. No Jew who could possibly travel to Jerusalem at this season was willing to miss the event. They came from vast distances; brought a lamb to be offered as a sacrifice; brought their temple tithes; brought whatever they had to sell in the markets. The city was gorged to suffocation with homing Jews. The bazaars were a riot of color and gay confusion.

Religion had this big flare-up seasonally. On ordinary days it plodded along dully, of no particular interest to anybody but the priests, who regarded it with stolid perfunctoriness. When the Passover came, religion was lighted up for a few hours and became suddenly invested with high significance.

Jesus was a strong advocate of a religion that did not need to have the oxygen pump applied to it every so often to keep it from dying. Let a man live in constant awareness of his spiritual oneness with his Father, and there would be no necessity of these frantic struggles, periodically, to renew people's interest in God.

Of course, it will not be becoming of us to ridicule the heavy commercializing of the Passover, whereby the feast had become an annual fête in which the ingredients were mixed on a basis of three parts religion to seven parts commerce. We go through much the same motions seasonally. We who see our churches jammed to the sidewalk on Easter morning, with huge crowds of gayly dressed people eager to compare their spring finery, have lost our ticket to criticize the Passover feast as it was enacted in Jerusalem. We who see our churches maneuvered into the spotlight for a few hours on Christmas Eve, when, by common consent, everybody grows mellow and sentimental about the advent of the Christ Child; when even the newspapers, who mostly have quite lost their souls and are become the most diabolical influence in present life, make place in their scandal-reeking, sodden, sordid, shameful pages for a grotesque reproduction of some early Roman Catholic painting of the Babe of Bethlehem— surely we ought to be able to understand the mood of the young Galilean as he sees these throngs of people milling through the streets of the Holy City on an occasion when religion was being used, temporarily, as an axis on which to spin their various pleasures and commercial affairs.

But we must not linger here too long. We have the frame for the picture now. There is a great feast.

Religion is having one of its periodical surges of activity. The angel is making one of his seasonal visits.

"Now there is in Jerusalem, by the Sheep Gate, a pool ——" Just a moment! Not so fast, please! Where have we heard of that "Sheep Gate" before? Oh yes; away back in the Book of Nehemiah. You remember how Nehemiah was rebuilding the walls around Jerusalem? He ordered every family to work on whatever segment of the wall was nearest to its house. It is recorded that Eliashib, the high priest, assisted by the other priests, rebuilt and hung the Sheep Gate. That means the official executive mansion of the high priest was hard by the Sheep Gate. Let us proceed:

"——by the Sheep Gate, a pool ——" Surely it does not take much exercise of the imagination to picture this old pool as the favorite rendezvous and recreation center for the holy brethren of the cloth. It was directly in front of their headquarters, and, doubtless, there they walked daily, solemnly intoning the sacred lore from the Pentateuch. By all means let us go ahead with this. It looks as if we have stumbled upon a clue to John's allegory. Read on:

"——a pool, which is called in Hebrew 'Bethesda,' having five porches ——" Wait a minute! Five porches! A pentagonal! The Pentateuch! To be sure, the old pool, in the very courtyard of the high priest's house, would have five porches. (It's a wonder

John did not set up twelve lamp-posts around this pavilion, to symbolize the twelve tribes of Israel. Perhaps he assumed that everybody would catch the idea of his picture by letting the matter rest with the five-porched pavilion.)

Is the situation clearing a little? John appears to be drawing an impressionistic sketch of the way Jesus viewed the old religion of his people. He sees a miniature of it in the Pool of Bethesda. It was natural he should have adopted this historic pool as an emblem of the Hebrew cultus because for a very long time it had been so closely identified with the priestly establishment. The pool, then, stands for the Israelitish established religion. Now and again this pool is stirred into activity. It is as if an angel touched it, and temporarily invested it with power. Thousands swarmed about it, periodically, hoping to receive certain benefits. But the very people who most desperately needed to be healed in its remedial waters were exactly the people who were elbowed aside. There stood the ancient institution, roofed over with the sacred traditions, and sporadically attracting public attention; but good only for the applicants who could help themselves. It had no hope to offer the downs-and-outs.

According to John's picture, Jesus' new gospel comes along and views the situation. It sets this particular type of needy soul free to find life abundant, elsewhere and otherwise than by gazing hungrily into the magic water that held out so very little promise to the man who could not meet its conditions.

Unquestionably there is a tremendous lesson here. How easily a religion goes to crystal! How quickly a religious cult walls its benefits in and erects a roof over its holy place. How readily it settles into a perfunctory grind of solemn festivals and stated ceremonials, which the most needy have the least chance of applying to their own pressing wants. The old dogmas! The old rites! What a trick they have of handling all problems except the really important problems of human life!

IV

Already the official leadership of the established religion was making plans to frustrate the Galilean in his liberty movement. At the hour, Caiaphas, the high priest, had spies out. One sympathizes with Caiaphas in the awkward position he occupied. He was the appointed chieftain of an institution which dreaded the introduction of new ideas. Its main ambition was to conserve its ancient traditions. It was an historic, rather than a prophetic, organization. For the future it gave no thought, and for the present it had only a sigh and a tear. Of the past it sang in requial respect. Oh, but those were the days, and that was the life, when King David sat on the throne. Even Solomon, for all that his reign had been conspicuous mostly for the increase of taxes and the inadequate housing facilities of the palace, where entirely too many idle people were living in luxury—even Solomon's day was now remembered as an era of great pomp and power. And back of the kings there had been mighty men of valor who had recaptured the Promised Land. Back of them Moses, who had defied a Pharaoh, had led a tatterdemalion host into freedom. Back of Moses the patriarchs moved wraithlike across the desert, mounted on their tall camels, plodding on toward a new and larger liberty.

Of all these historic emancipations, the priests chanted daily in the temple; and from these remembered quests of liberty the people were enjoined to deduce their religious satisfactions. Jehovah belonged to the past. Not lately had He spoken. Now He sat watching the scattered remnant of a once proud and successful race in its efforts to keep a league ahead of actual starvation and resignedly accept the humiliations put upon it by its foreign master. Such religion as there was, consequently, made no attempt to be an aspiration, but only a reminiscence. The temple was not a school of spiritual advancement, but a monument to a nation's lost youth, a veritable mausoleum where holy men in ornate vestments stood solemn watch about the casket of a dead issue.

Seeing this was the real aim and mission of the temple—to safeguard these ancient relics and traditions—it was quite disturbing when a new idea began to filter through the current social order, looking toward a moral and spiritual emancipation from the tyranny of old bones and the murky atmosphere of old legends. Caiaphas knew that his institution was not rigged to accommodate itself to a new idea—this one or any other. It is hard to rebuild a mausoleum into anything other than what it is. The high priest knew that the temple could never be made over to fit a quest for freedom. Either the temple must go on, without a single modification, or go utterly into the discard. When, therefore, Jesus of Nazareth proposes a better way for men to live than in the fear of ancient thou-shalt-nots; when he offered a way of altruistic service and universal brotherhood, a general breaking down of the old divisive walls of caste and color and creed— Caiaphas knew that either this new voice must be silenced or the established religion would crumble. He plans the cross as the one imperative to the safety of the temple.

But history has a way of repeating itself. Religion is always *en route* to a predicament exactly like that in which old Caiaphas found his. Strangely enough, it is when an organized religion is engaged in its youthful struggle that it makes its greatest contribution to spiritual culture. Once it has built high walls about itself and the walls are covered with ivy; once it has evolved a settled way of doing things and has standardized its work and worship until its chief pride is the antiquity of the date on its cornerstone; once it has become a place where the touring buses stop and the guides declaim—then you may expect that somewhere in the very vicinity of this obsolescent enterprise, probably under its very eaves, there will be a little excavation started which, before it is done, will have marked the beginning of an edifice ten times more important than the old one.

Whenever a religious institution arrives at perfection and admits that it has now found all the light necessary to a proper view of its tasks, then it is time for a youth movement.

Caiaphas was ready to indict Jesus as an ingrate, turning from the religion of his fathers, inviting men to find new life and health otherwise than at the old pool under its pentagonal pavilion; but it is to be observed that liberty movements are always born in the very shadow of an obsolete cause. Savonarola did not come romping into Florence from some foreign country, to say to the old Church that it stood greatly in need of a return to a lost morality. Savonarola was a nonconforming product of the Church, bone of her bone, flesh of her flesh. Luther was not an alien, migrating into Germany to inform the intellectuals that Christian dogmatism required a reappraisal. He was a child of the Church. Jesus of Nazareth was not a noisy scoffer who, with no interest in or concern for the established religion of his day, bombarded it as a stranger. He was a devotee of that faith. The earliest memories he had were of trips to Jerusalem with his parents to pay tribute and offer sacrifice in the hallowed temple.

He did not go down to the Pool of Bethesda, that Sabbath morning, to grin at the fatuity of the enterprise. He regarded that situation with deep sorrow and regret. Here lay, on the flagging, a short cross-section of current society. The pool was good for a therapeutic bath if a man was on his feet. It had nothing to offer the man who was helpless.

There is a great truth implied by this story. Let contemporaneous Christianity, as administered by our churches, take note. Our institutions are already old, in the ranks of so-called Protestantism. Are we adaptable to the new thoughts which insist upon receiving attention? Are we merely maintaining historic old pools, beautifully roofed over with traditional symbolisms and venerated lore? Have we made suitable provision for the type of humanity that most seriously needs the encouragement and consolation of the gospel? Is it true that when the angel stirs the waters occasionally, the only people who benefit are they whose lives are already filled with privilege? That charge is openly made. Is it true?

V

Let us examine a few cases directly in point. How about the poor man who excited so much of Jesus' sympathy and interest? What does he think of religion, today? Under our imposing pentagonals, he realizes the hopelessness of his ever getting exactly what he

wants. Occasionally some roaming prophet comes along
and advertises a big religious show; rents a hall; fills
it nightly with wind and confusion; draws pictures of
a lurid hell and its screeching host of victims; ex-
coriates everything that the intellectual and moral leadership of the community has done and is doing to make
the place easier to live in; hoots at all beliefs but the
constricted superstitions of his own frantic sect; and
lays a hypnotic spell upon the masses whose emotions
are not very well disciplined. On such husks are the
poor feeding, today, who inquire for the bread of life.
Or, to get back to John's picture, the old pool isn't able
to take care of these cases which most urgently cry out
for help. The respectable go down into it; the general
riffraff stay out.

Jesus' gospel was a kindly call to these wretched
people to come out from under the old roof and away
from the old pool, to find salvation through an active
faith in a few high principles. Let all the churches that
have settled into a satisfied acceptance of conventional
routine and the rotund intonation of ponderous phrases,
keep this story of Jesus' miracle at the Pool of Bethesda
in plain sight.

Again; how about the man who has become so bewildered on the subject of religion that he knows not which
way to turn? He goes to the old pool, and is told that
he must go down into it, in a stated way and at a given
time. He must sit under the eaves of the Pentateuch,
or its modern equivalent. Here's the good old Book,

says the parson. Believe it and live. It is interesting to note that only an hour after Jesus' experience at the Pool of Bethesda, in reply to the critics who queried him about his attitude toward it, he said, "Ye search the scriptures, for ye think that in them ye have eternal life."

One of the most urgent calls that ever can be made upon the Church for high benefits is on the occasion when death has invaded a home and swept away its dearest possession. The Church had done much talking about death as a mere incident to the acquisition of a better and freer life. On Easter, the choir had sung "Unfold, Ye Portals," "Alleluia," "For All the Saints Who from Their Labors Rest." Flowers, symbolic of immortality, were banked about the chancel in rich profusion. The preacher reached a pinnacle of eloquence. Happy people, gayly attired, went out of the place telling one another it was the most inspiring and helpful service they had ever attended. It was certain the angel had touched the pool that morning, albeit the people who went down into it were not very seriously in need of its remedial waters.

Now, there is a desperate situation to be faced. Death is not now something to be apostrophized in brave phrases, and melodiously extolled by the choir as the agency that sets men free. This time it is a terrible enemy, swift, silent, mysterious.

There is a funeral. The neighbors come in and spend an uncomfortable half hour in a badly ventilated, overcrowded house. The people who most desperately need help are tucked away somewhere upstairs. A collection of sonorous sentences are read out of a black book. The whole situation is stiff, tense, and stagey. People tiptoe about and speak in whispers. The blinds are drawn. After a while the dull little drama is over and a solemn procession loads up and moves off to the cemetery. Some more ponderous observations are read from the black book—"Ashes to ashes, earth to earth, dust to dust." Everybody can get into the pool but the people who most need it. The angel is not working today.

John's picture brings us up with a start. Perhaps no single episode recorded of the Master's life so plainly warns against the tendency of organized religion to achieve such a wealth of standardized dignity and self-conscious power that it fails, in strategic moments, to hold out hope and blessing for those whose problems are not to be solved by the recitation of ancient maxims; whose sufferings are not to be relieved by the protecting shelter of symbolic roofs.

CHAPTER TEN

THE COSTLY MIRACLES

I

NOTWITHSTANDING the primary purpose of our study thus far has been a quest of the "overtones" in the ancient minstrelsy relating to the wonder deeds of the Master, it might properly be considered an omission if we failed to take account of his many ministries of healing and helpfulness concerning which no such interpretation is permissible.

After all the conjectures have been made on the spiritual lessons presumably hidden beneath the surface of the text in these venerable records, an important question still remains unconsidered until we have frankly addressed ourselves to the actual problem of Jesus' dealings with the sick.

Much light may be thrown upon this dilemma by making a brief survey of the healing power of the Jesus culture at the present hour. Let his message of hope be borne today to some benighted island and set to work in the untamed minds of savages; it will be only a short time until these creatures are trying to grow flowers beside their doorsteps and teaching their little children fair play and better manners. Draw a map of progressive civilization, and you have drawn a map of Christendom. Find the important centers of the world's highest achievements in scientized altruism, and you have found the localities where Christianity is of largest interest in the popular mind.

To account for this survival of a Personality, through all the radical changes experienced by civilization in the past two millennia, on the ordinary grounds by which one explains the spiritual persistence of a Francis Bernardone, a Cavour, a Wesley, or a Lincoln, is as futile as to attempt to trace the sea anemone and the date palm to a common origin by virtue of the fact that they both have waving fronds. The Jesus influence is different from all other motivations, not only quantitatively, but qualitatively. In the name of George Washington, men may be challenged to a deeper patriotism; in the name of Jesus, men are called into a complete newness of life whereby their outlook upon all the considerations of human existence is changed as if by a miracle of re-creation.

Surely no one needs be told what a regnant, enveloping, masterly human personality can do to influence the thought, feelings, and conduct of other people who have confidence in the wisdom and integrity of such leadership. There is no doubt about the reality of these influences as exerted every day in our normal relationships—the influence of the physician over his patient, the teacher over his student, the mother over her child.

In seeking to learn something of the probable nature

of Jesus' command over the lives he touched at close range in Galilee and Judæa, let us multiply the best that any modern man has ever achieved in the field of personality projection, by as much as may be thought a just and honest tribute to the one Super-personality who, today, towers majestically above any other influence in the world; a Master personality who, at this hour, after all the sifting and testing of the ages, stands supreme as the most important force in modern life. Deduce the obvious conclusion. What effect might his actual presence have wrought upon the troubled minds of his own contemporaries?

If Jesus had enough personal dynamics to become the greatest single urge and inspiration to mankind, vitalizing people with hope, courage, and self-sacrifice, today—seven thousand miles and nearly two thousand years remote—what manner of grip do you think he might have had upon the will and imagination of the man who sat *across the table from him?*

It is said that a woman, suffering a disease in which her general neural equipment was heavily involved, shyly touched his robe and was instantly cured. There is nothing incredible about this. People who find the story hard to believe are not very well posted on what is happening daily in psychiatric clinics. One's faith must be very feeble indeed (and one's experience and observation of contemporaneous achievements in the field of suggestive therapeutics extremely limited) if one is disposed to doubt the tremendous effect of such assurance as must have been spoken from the lips of one so thoroughly *en rapport* with his spiritual Source that he had become wholly independent of fear, hate, deceit, and all the rest of the inherited psychogenic weaknesses which, to a greater or less degree, cloud the radiation of our own personalities.

Did Jesus heal the sick? Assuredly! Why not? Could a Personality with a reach and grasp long and strong enough to command the world's progress in altruism, across the centuries, accomplish anything remedial by direct contact, at a bedside—*his hand upon the patient's brow?*

We self-confessed "modernists" must have a care lest, in our honest and commendable endeavor to relieve the Galilean's story of its magical features—in the interest of reconciling it with what we think we know about the orderly outworking of natural laws in a law-abiding universe under the direction of an apparently law-loving God—we fail to take account of the fact that the Jesus personality so overwhelmingly transcends any other personality ever known in the world that comparisons drawn between him and other men only make the others, however useful and dynamic, seem mere pygmies dwarfed to insignificance in his presence.

Of course, after the Jesus era is over and most of the first-hand witnesses of his deeds are gone; when the memorabilia are being tardily collected for future preservation, many reports—by this time crystallized into definite legends—are likely to deal all too fancifully with the actual facts. It must be remembered that in the early apostolic days the end of the world was momentarily expected, and no attempt was made to put the records of Jesus' words and works into permanent form. He himself wrote nothing; nor have we any word of a request or desire on his part that pains should be taken to see to the production of an informative literature concerning him, for future use.

Belatedly, then, the stories were compiled, from various sources, relative to the Master's deeds. It is not only natural that a considerable amount of the legendary had already tinctured the facts : it would have been an astounding situation if that were not so. Nor does this imply a willful intention to deceive, on the part of the faithful men and women who heard and told these tales. We are all aware of the ease with which the most healthy and honest minds distill their perceptions, producing strange compounds of fact and fancy so inextricably mixed that even they themselves are unable to state the exact proportions of the elements combined in the solution.

Persons of sound mind and a disposition to be truthful have gone, out of sheer curiosity, to visit a fortune teller. In the course of the interview certain cryptic statements are made by the seeress which may, at that moment, mean this, that, or the other; like the ancient Delphian oracles. Little attention is paid to the forecasts of the fortune teller, and no credence is given to them. Months pass. Epochal events, possibly of a tragic nature, arise in the experience of one of these people who had consulted the prophet. Now everything that was revealed of the future, on that occasion, becomes swiftly illuminated and fraught with high significance. Marvelous! The story of that interview is told and retold, again and again, to awe-stricken groups. It gets bigger and better in the telling. It comes to you, perhaps, after its evolution is quite complete. You hear your friends—presumably of normal mind and an inclination to be truthful—reciting this strange tale with all the zeal and unction of believers willing to be martyred for their cause. It baffles you. You decide that either they have gone stark mad or you have.

I have personally known of men and women whose mental capacity and integrity could not have been surpassed by any Galilean fisherman of two thousand years ago who, at spiritualistic séances, actually heard the voices of their lately departed loved ones; listened to their reminiscences of facts which the medium could not have known; came out of the place sworn devotees of spiritualism; told their remarkable experiences to intimate friends, in a spirit of deep faith, even growing a bit impatient over the reluctance of their friends to accept, at face value, these strange reports of their hand-to-hand grapple with the Other World.

I have known these same people to lose all interest in such endeavors, and utterly disavow their belief in the reality of such communications.

The human imagination is a very interesting and

highly unreliable institution, and that general observation goes for the most honest and trustworthy people in the world. Let us keep this fact in mind as we review the records of all wonder deeds ever wrought— the deeds of Jesus not excluded.

The Master meets a man with a "withered" hand; tells him to stretch forth the deformed hand; restores it, with a word, to normal size. What are we to think of this? Doubtless all miracles of this type are to be studied with a sympathetic understanding of the circumstances under which these records were collected. An event like this cannot be accounted for on the ground of a dominant personality in action, be it ever so dominant. The "withered hand" miracle is an excellent example of the sort of wonder tale which permits no explanation whatsoever. It is there in the Book; you take it or leave it.

Pathology is well acquainted, however, with the clinical records of many cases in which an urgent motive has recreated an impotent will. The outbreak of a fire in a hospital has occasionally cured physical difficulties rooted in a psychopathic condition. A shock has frequently disposed of an otherwise incurable aphasia, so that persons who had not spoken normally, or at all, for years, have regained what they had lost. Religious conversion has again and again restored the health of people suffering of ills traceable to neurasthenic conditions. One sees no reason for doubting the very considerable field of usefulness open to a man whose personality was as a radiant, glowing, commanding, kinetic energy! Did Jesus relieve Peter's wife's mother of her fever? Why not, indeed? Did he cure all manner of sickness, and tell helpless invalids to get up off their beds and walk? Why doubt it?

II

Conspicuous among the maladies which Jesus is said to have cured one finds the strange psychopathic condition known as "demoniacal possession."

This is no place to go into the study of demonology. It is too long. Anybody who wishes to be better informed about ancient belief in devils should consult the abundant literature on that subject. We may assume that in Jesus' time the phrase "demoniacal possession" was a quick and easy diagnosis of abnormal mental conditions, not otherwise explicable.

The Master is almost daily "casting out devils." Did he himself believe in "demoniacal possession"? Very likely. Everybody else did. Why not he?

We must be careful in our thinking about the nature of Jesus' prescience. It seems entirely permissible to believe that the Master could confidently forecast what would occur in the world of the future if any considerable number of men adopted as their code of life the program comprehended by "the Golden Rule." He can predict, with startling accuracy, what will come to pass if certain conditions obtain. When, however, we impute to him a gift of prescience which enables him to comprehend facts not only undiscovered at the time with which he is associated, but undiscoverable until a long period of experimentation and research shall have opened the way to such information, we immediately gift him with an omniscience which removes him, automatically, from the position of an "exemplar" to us.

The chief problem with which we humans have to contend is the almost utter lack of our knowledge concerning the future. We have had enough experience to justify our belief that the sun will rise tomorrow morning; that a certain type of weather is indicated by the season of the year; that given causes will produce definitely guaranteed effects. But, because we do not know whether we will live the day through, or what emergencies will arise, our decisions are made in the dark. If we knew in advance exactly what penalties would fall on our heads for certain infractions of moral laws, we could be depended upon to avoid doing things that would menace our peace and jeopardize our welfare. In other words, any man with the gift of prescience, able to see in advance the effects of any choice he makes today upon his happiness and success tomorrow or ten years from tomorrow, never confronted with dilemmas because possessed of prophetic insight—such a man would find it difficult to request normal people, unendowed with this strange forecasting vision, to believe as he believes and behave as he behaves.

It will be safer to predicate of Jesus the mind of a

normal man, in respect to future events. If he is able to announce, a few days before his tragedy, that the forces which are converging to bring him to disaster are now arriving at sharp focus, he can deduce such a belief from the facts at hand. If he is able to predict the downfall of the city of Jerusalem, in the near future, he can see that crisis coming as a result of conditions entirely apparent to a discerning eye. But if we permit him a prescience which puts him, in comprehension of pathology, out of his own generation, and ahead of his epoch by several hundreds of years, we do violence to the very greatest purpose he serves us —his capacity as a moral leader and example.

We presume, therefore, that Jesus accepted the general belief of his day in "demoniacal possession." If he did not believe it, one finds it strange that he countenanced it. There was a common belief that devils inhabited certain unfortunate individuals; lived in them; fed off of them, after the manner of an ichneumon fly in the vitals of a caterpillar; motivated them; spoke for them. We may conjecture that some of these "possessions" were psychoses. Doubtless the phrase, "demoniacal possession," was often used very loosely; for we hear of "dumb devils"; though muteness, of all misfortunes, by its very calmness was obviously not the work of devils.

We are aware that present-day psychiatry is able to do a great deal for certain types of obsession and other mental disorders, by means of suggestion. A dominating personality, by the use of firm and friendly counsel, administered in authoritative tones, can and does accomplish remarkable results in putting disheveled minds to rights. If this be true in the experience of our own work in psychiatry, how much more spectacular may have been the personal influence of Jesus on such cases!

Among the stories we have of the Master's dealing with men possessed of demons, the most elaborately detailed is the report of the exorcism wrought upon the wild man of Gadara.

Any one who insists it is pure guesswork on our part to say that Jesus was eager to learn what reactions might be produced by his gospel on the minds of widely different social groups, is correct. Whoever says it is a mere assumption of ours that the Galilean went to Gadara to ascertain whether his discoveries of life's imperatives could be effectually communicated to a benighted, stolid, unaspiring province—for such Gadara unquestionably was—wins the debate. It is frequently implied, however, that Jesus was tremendously concerned with the impression his gospel was making upon people of various temperaments. "Whom do men say that I am?" was not asked in solicitation of flattery, but information. Even at the last minute, in Pilate's private office, he permits a very precious opportunity for self-defense to go by, while he endeavors to learn whether the Roman Procurator had any definite ideas on the nature of spiritual leadership. You may recall the interview.

Pilate to Jesus: "Art thou a king?"

Jesus to Pilate: "Sayest thou this of thyself, or did others tell it thee?"

At all events, and for whatever purpose, Jesus goes to benighted Gadara, only a little distance in terms of miles, but, every other way considered, a foreign country, a poor, bare, ignorant, selfish, sour, and sullen land, obviously in great need of a new hope and a high ideal to lift its people out of their degradation.

He was there only a few hours. The Gadarenes were practically unanimous in their request that he depart. Their reason for asking him to leave was that his benefits were too expensive. The full story is intensely interesting; at certain turns a bit grotesque; in a few particulars quite incredible; but on the whole a most rewarding study.

Jesus' experience in the country of the Gadarenes is easily and briefly recited. Upon arrival by boat with his disciples, the Master is confronted by a madman who comes roaring out of the tombs, near the coast, making menacing gestures. The lunatic is possessed of devils which have him so completely in charge that they are able to speak for him. The demons recognize Jesus as the Son of God; beg him not to exorcise them; but, feeling sure he is about to do so, request that they be sent into yonder herd of swine feeding on the shoulder of a neighboring cliff. The Master humors their wish.

The difficulties of a literal acceptance of this phase of the story are serious and obvious. If we are to consent to "demoniacal possession," we must insist that the phrase be used merely by accommodation. If it is employed in a purely rhetorical manner, all well and good. But when these alleged "devils" are objectified, and dealt with on a basis of their actual reality—transferred, by command, from the body of a man to the bodies of swine—we must demur. Else—conceding the actuality of "demons"—we confess belief that our God is in competition with a great malevolent Rival, which rather effectually destroys our faith in God's omnipotence and sends us forth to seek a Universal Power who *is* independent of any competing Spirit.

Moreover, Jesus' readiness to comply with the wishes of a "legion of demons" does such small credit to his fearlessness, that we find the episode too fanciful for acceptance. We are not disposed to believe that Jesus had any traffic with "devils," much less assumed a conciliatory attitude toward them, to the extent of respecting and obeying their suggestions.

According to the story, however, the demons, at Jesus' command, enter the swine. The herd scurries violently over the cliff into the sea. The swineherds rush to the near-by town to report the disaster. The whole population turns out, finding Jesus and the erstwhile lunatic seated in quiet conversation. All the people are amazed over the dangerous man's restoration to sanity. Gadara is plentifully supplied with unfortunate people who would be vastly improved if this remarkable healer could be persuaded to remain and relieve them of their devils. The general public wishes that all the lunatics, and other jeopardies to the health and safety of the community, might be restored. But there was no getting past the fact that this one cure had cost a whole herd of swine. No telling what might be the extent of the economic losses to Gadara, as the price of the salvation they so greatly desired. The swine-owners were surest of all that Jesus' ministrations might prove too expensive. So "they besought him to depart out of their coasts."

However grotesque certain phases of this legend may sound, it provides a very significant illustration of the economic cost of accepting the gospel as a working hypothesis, reminding one of the two brothers in the coal business, one of whom professed conversion during a high-pressure "revival"; the other, no less disposed to accept salvation, was obliged to suppress his worthy desire, inasmuch as both agreed that somebody must be left in the firm who could weigh the coal undeterred by any embarrassing inhibitions laid on by a gospel enjoining an immaculate honesty.

Plenty of instances might be cited. Whole communities have refused to accept some guaranteed remedy for their social problems, on the ground of its expense. It is utterly foolish to spread the gospel with any propaganda calculated to create an impression that it is to be had for nothing. The rumor that "salvation is free" appeals to frugal minds who endeavor to confirm the fallacy by the parsimonious policies they advocate for the conduct of religious and philanthropic organizations. One of the finest testimonies to the divine guidance exercised over the Church is the bare fact that only by supernatural intervention could it have survived the niggardly support it has received from its own adherents.

One of the most expensive of the luxuries is the Golden Rule. A half-hearted practice of it is dangerous. To patch up damaged humanity to the point where it may breed more delinquents and deficients is to do the social order a distinct disservice, unless there accompanies such restoration the processes of character-building which will make these physical reclamations worth the bother; and character-building processes are very costly.

Jesus stands ready to help Gadara. "But how about these hogs?" inquire the Gadarenes.

III

One of the most delightful examples of Jesus' ability to transform something into something else appears in the well-remembered story of the miracle he performed upon Zacchæus. We turn to it with pleasure, as exactly the right thing to take the taste out of our mouths after studying the case of the low-geared Gadarenes.

Perhaps an objection may be raised to the effect that Jesus' operation on Zacchæus was not, strictly speaking, a miracle. Some people are not content with a miracle unless it involves an act that is, on the face of it, incredible. They like the sensation of stoutly declaring that they are able to believe something completely out of the customary beat of human experience. They do not consider the Master's effect upon Zacchæus as a miracle. If the mean little rascal had been blind and Jesus had said some words that restored his sight, that would have been a miracle indeed. But for Jesus merely to transform this wicked grafter, who had stolen from his neighbors until he did not have a friend in town, into a generous, high-minded, public-spirited citizen— that may not be counted a miracle. We think it is all of that—a miracle!

Jesus is passing through Jericho. The streets are gorged, for the Galilean's fame has preceded him and everybody is out, standing on tiptoe to see him. The crowd has waited a long time, and now a stir, up the avenue, indicates that he is coming at last. There is much craning of necks and treading upon toes.

There was a decidedly unpopular little Jew in Jericho by the name of Zacchæus. To say that everybody in the city despised him is merely to be saying nothing whatsoever concerning the esteem in which he was held by his fellow townsmen. Zacchæus was the revenue officer, in the employ of the Roman government. That position, even if a man were scrupulously honest in it, was sufficient to make him a social outcast. But Zacchæus was not only disloyal to his own race in that he was willing to serve a greedy foreign state as a local representative; he was an embezzler and an extortionist. And all the people in Jericho knew it.

Zacchæus heard that Jesus was coming, and desired to see him. The fact that he knew himself to be the best hated man in Jericho did not deter the diminutive cheat from scrambling for an excellent position to view the Nazarene's approach. Zacchæus had all the brass in the world. Dark looks and guttural curses meant nothing to him. He was accustomed to these displays of his fellow citizens' regard for him. He climbed into the spreading branches of a sycamore tree, where he could see everything, indifferent to the fact that his fortuitous position invited the unfriendly comment of his neighbors.

Jesus pauses beneath the tree and calls Zacchæus down. It had been a long time since anybody had spoken to him except in open scorn. He swung down from the tree and walked beside the Galilean at the head of the procession. Now he will show these snobbish people that he really is somebody, after all. It was a great day for little Zacchæus. With what glowing swank and swagger does he march along, taking great strides to measure his step to that of his new-found friend from Galilee! And Jesus is going home with him to dinner! Zacchæus will show off all his fine plate, bought with money wrung from the thin purses of his neighbors.

But the dinner did not turn out exactly as Zacchæus had planned. He tried to be debonair and act the perfect host, but he found himself flinching under the calm but searching inquiry of those penetrating eyes that bored through the thick shell of him and into the most sensitive plexus of his sick soul. When dinner was over, Zacchæus rose and announced in the presence of enough people to guarantee against the possibility of retraction, that he would pay back, fourfold, all the money he had taken unlawfully. Half of his wealth he would give to the poor. Jesus' only comment was, "Salvation has come today to this house." He did not add that salvation was free. Zacchæus had not achieved his at bargain rates. He was prepared to pay. One feels that Zacchæus had a very real conversion and that he fully understood what the gospel was about. It had made him honest and socially minded. Nothing short of a miracle could have done it!

IV

We turn now to the tale of a wondrous deed that must have been costly for Jesus. It was wrought upon his foe.

Perhaps the most seriously neglected miracle story is the episode in which Malchus loses an ear. Four gospels report that on the tragic night when Jesus was arrested in Gethsemane, one Malchus, the high priest's servant, was injured. When the mob accosted the Master, Peter drew his sword and slashed wildly about with it. Before Jesus had had time to forbid this show of resistance, Malchus had lost his right ear. One gathers that the only reason the story is told is to point to the fact that Jesus preferred not to be defended. He rebukes Peter and commands him to sheathe his sword.

Three of the gospels merely note Malchus' injury, and pass on. Luke, however, states that Jesus touched the wound and healed it. Be that as it may. We like the idea, anyway. Jesus expresses his sympathy and concern for this wounded man. Did he heal the wounded ear by magic? What matters it? All we care to know about it is the bare fact that Jesus was concerned for Malchus.

Of course, if the Master had said, "That's what you get for coming out here in a crowd of ruffians to do a cruel thing to a man who had never done you any harm!"—there is not an honest man in the world who could say that the remark was otherwise than true, just, and well deserved.

Jesus has a perfect right to say, "You have had your pay for meddling in something that did not concern you. I had never interfered with your pleasure, your liberty, or your property. You did not know me. You came here because you wanted to do some violence upon a stranger, believing you would be safe in a mob arrayed against a little group of weaponless men. Peter did wrong in drawing the sword; but, as for you, the punishment was in order."

We are privileged to believe that Jesus does not stop to inquire critically how a man may have come by his hurts. The fact that he is hurt looms up so large that the circumstances under which he was hurt are driven into complete eclipse.

Here is a miracle that needs to be recommended to all the followers of Jesus, everywhere. There is all too little of good sportsmanship displayed by the self-confessed disciples of the Master. They are a bit short, sometimes, in magnanimity. They are willing to give of what they have, but they like to make certain that the object of their generosity is "worthy." Frequently they ask the beggar who solicits alms how he came by his misfortune. Well, it's reasonably sure he didn't come by it through thrift or industry, and, now that he is in this sorry predicament, does it matter so much how he managed to arrive in this plight? The only fact worth noting is the present misery of him. However he came by it, here he is with it. One feels that Jesus, as a social investigator, pursuing the modern technique of analysis by the case method, would be a doubtful success. Without question, the chief executive of the Associated Charities, after having Jesus on his staff of investigators for one day, would either put him in some other department or let him out altogether.

Here is one legend that deserves posting in all the

offices where we examine the battered members of society to see if they really should be given aid. For sometimes scientized altruism is a bit more intent upon its orderly files, and the correct codification of its statistics, than the actual alleviation of suffering.

Great ecclesiastical conventions occasionally stage militant debates, full of bitterness and contempt. Charges and countercharges are batted back and forth. Magnanimity seems strangely lacking. What a wonderful motto to paint on a banner and suspend over the tempest: "REMEMBER THE EAR OF MALCHUS!"

How proud one may be of one's Christian idealism, generated by a Personality so far above the petty desires for revenge and reprisal that he can deal tenderly and sympathetically with a man who has come, not as a suppliant, but as an assassin!

It may be presumed that some of Jesus' ministries of helpfulness cost more than others. We can understand how easy and pleasant it may have been to feed the five thousand. But to minister to the wound of a man who had come out to deal cruelly with him, in the dark—this miracle must have been very costly.

CHAPTER ELEVEN

MISTAKEN FOR THE GARDENER

I

JUST how far a purely speculative investigation like ours may presume to go, in a search for the "overtones" in the stories told of Jesus' resurrection from the tomb, without inviting the charge that we are flippant meddlers with a venerated epic which permits no such liberties, is a disturbing question.

Whoever feels that this query should have been decided in the negative has so many excellent points on his side that he will doubtless do himself a good turn by omitting this chapter, on the ground that he does not wish to be unnecessarily irritated over the presumption.

Our only reason for going into the matter at all is based upon the fact that many good people are already so seriously disturbed over the resurrection story that it is unlikely our interpretation can add anything to their confusion, while we take at least a slim chance of relieving it a little.

Christianity, as an institution, was founded upon the firm belief of a small group of loyal and fearless disciples of Jesus that their Master rose from the dead. Faith in that astounding event was considered, from the very earliest days of the Church, as the *sine qua non* of Christian belief. Let us make no mistake concerning the regard in which this doctrine was held in the apostolic period. There were many points of controversy among the leaders of the early Christian Church, but this was not one of them.

Paul went to the length of saying that if Jesus did not rise from the dead, all Christian teaching was useless and all Christian hope was vain. These strong words were in answer to the evident reluctance of many persons to accept the doctrine of their own ultimate resurrection. Paul adds that if this Christian tenet be denied, one might as well "eat and drink"—a stock phrase of the Epicurean, connoting complete abandonment to pleasure.

Of course, we are not required to consent to the Pauline logic at this particular point. It is not so sure, as the Tarsan seemed to think, that a disbelief in resurrection leaves a program of selfishness and debauchery as one's natural alternative. If some document were exhumed, today, offering indubitable testimony that the story of Jesus' resurrection was untrue, it is to be doubted if a general collapse would occur to our common morality. Quite too much has been made of the eventualities of this doctrine in its effect upon human character and conduct. Indeed, we have strong grounds for believing that very few persons, per hundred thousand, would offer, as an excuse for their sins, the breakdown of their faith in resurrection. The Jews had contrived to do without that hope, and were the moral mentors of the world—a fact which Paul well knew. Our own guess about the loose relation of the doctrine of the resurrection to humanity's morals is premised on the fact that a very large number of law-abiding, generous, sober, and cultured people do live circumspectly, albeit unsupported by a belief in resurrection—Jesus' or any other's.

However, in the face of such a volume of strong conviction on the subject of the resurrection, the present-day Christian who boldly documents his disbelief in the story has aligned himself against a faith so well established and widely maintained that his dissent seems but an impertinent effrontery.

Notwithstanding, modern processes of reasoning are making it a bit easier for people to express their doubts, even concerning matters presumed to be quite beyond the reach of inquiry. Recent studies of the manner in which our minds operate have led to the growing conviction, on the part of many psychologists, that one has not only a right, but a duty, to view with a critical eye the essential soundness of any belief which, when the light of research makes a gesture of turning in its direction, impressively raises holy hands and shouts, "Sacrosanct!" Whenever a dogma has arrived at the stage of self-assurance where it denies an honest inquirer the right to ask questions about it, immediately a strong desire overwhelms the student to peek through the keyhole and attempt to learn what it is that the doctrine feels under compulsion to hide from the vulgar gaze of the curious.

We may assume that if the resurrection story is entirely sound and credible, it has nothing to fear from anybody's questions. We will further assume that it not only permits, but invites, investigation, as any self-respecting institution should, serenely conscious of its own integrity.

II

Certain peculiar facts need to be borne in mind respecting the mood of the early Christians in its bearing upon a correct interpretation of our Master's essential errand in this world.

The sacred art of four or five centuries ago, much of it very fortunately preserved, may be said to reflect the mind of the typical Christian of the early days; for the artists objectified conceptions of Christ which had been held, practically from the beginning, unto their own day—a time prior to any hint of an active revolt against the literal truth of a maze of tradition. This tradition had been bequeathed from generation to generation with practically no important changes. There were gradual accretions, but the embellishments were largely matters of minor detail, unaffecting the general structure of Christian belief.

These ancient pictures may be said to indicate the thought of the early Christians in regard to the main issues of Jesus' career as they evaluated them. It is to be observed that there are two major themes treated by the artists, almost to the exclusion of other incidents in the story of the Master. These two events are his birth and his death.

The conservative has the facts to support him if he explains this on the ground that fully twenty per cent of the sum total of gospel literature is occupied with a treatment of the nativity and the tragedy. On the other hand, it is quite worth mentioning that if the artists spend ninety per cent of their genius and time on events relating to twenty per cent of the gospels' narratives, is considerably out of drawing.

But one suspects that the artists' conception of Jesus was largely influenced, not by the gospels, but by a theology arrived at in ecclesiastical councils. That theology, briefly summarized, staked its claims on the following assumptions. When the human race was created in Eden, by divine fiat, the first man was informed that he would die on the day he broke a certain law. He promptly broke that law, and continued to live. The delay of execution was demanded by the fact that if Adam perishes, the whole unbegotten human race perishes with him. Adam is permitted to live that he may beget a posterity.

This left Jehovah in the disquieting predicament of having made a statement which lacked adequate fulfillment—a serious reflection upon the divine integrity. So, to make right this abrogation of justice, it was arranged that "in the fullness of time," God's Son would become incarnate and die in Adam's stead. This would "atone" for the temporary lapse of the law's enforcement in the first man's case, and legalize humanity's right to live. To speak in the practical terms of our present knowledge of such transactions, the whole enterprise of human civilization, from Adam to Jesus, was in the hands of a receiver, with a settlement pending.

Whatever frail warrant the theologians had for this ingenious belief was deduced mostly from the metaphysics of Paul, who was eager to convince the Jews that Jesus was sacrificed in much the same manner and for exactly the same purpose as the lamb on the altar. For ages, Jehovah's nostrils had been pleasantly stimulated by the savor of burning meat offered by men who were doing what little they could to win His favor. Now a sacrifice would be made, by His own Son, which would make complete redemption of the race.

It is obvious, then, that the theologians of the early Church premised a Christ who had come into the world for the specific purpose of dying. He was the Paschal Lamb; and, like the innocent creature of which he was the divine prototype, there was nothing for him to do but await the knife. His earthly days were spent in a patient anticipation of the strategic hour when he would justify his being in the world.

Here, then, is the explanation of the all-eclipsing portrait of a bleeding Christ, a pitiable innocent slaughtered in the interest of restoring to humanity its right to live. It accounts, as well, for the pageantry of the picture depicting his incarnation; for, second in importance to his death, is his birth.

In view of this doctrine of "the atonement," it is not difficult to understand how preëminently the last hours of Jesus loom up in traditional Christian thought; how vast a concern has been manifested over the minutest details of the trials, the sad march to Golgotha, the harrowing incidents involved in the crucifixion, and the circumstances of the entombment.

Had it been understood that Jesus was here primarily as a teacher of a new way of living, the heavy stress of Christian thought might have been laid upon the Sermon on the Mount, the circumstances of its delivery, and the effect of it upon the mind and conduct of its auditors.

Seeing, however, that Jesus' chief function is to die, everything directly or indirectly related to his tragedy appears in so high a relief that his active ministry of education and moral example rests in shadow.

This ancient theology is not quite content, however, to trace the sacrificial Lamb to a tomb, and close the sublime tragedy by rolling a stone against its open door. Once Jesus has "paid the price," he is free to go his way. The "redemptive" work accomplished, he may take up his life again.

At this point, in the opinion of many thoughtful people, the logic of the "atonement" theory is seriously disturbed in the interest of arriving at a happy eventuality.

Adam had been sentenced to die for his sin. It is not expressly stated in Genesis what fate would befall Adam's soul in the event he was executed for his crime, but one suspects annihilation is implied. Indeed, the promise made to Adam, contingent upon his being permitted to carry on for the sake of posterity, did not guarantee his soul's survival, if we may deduce anything from the statement, "Dust thou art, and unto dust shalt thou return." Adam's expectation of immortality was not fraught with much assurance, if we are to take seriously the declaration, "And Jehovah said, 'Behold, the man is become as one of us, to know good and evil; and now, lest he put forth his hand, and take also of the tree of life, and eat, and live forever'— therefore Jehovah God sent him forth from the garden. . . ."

Now, if Christ has come into the world, as the older theology declares, to take the place of Adam, and lose his life, he would better lose it, as Adam would have lost his, and let the matter rest there, without the dramatic sequel in which the life, instead of being lost, is merely put down for a brief interval between Friday afternoon and Sunday morning. Indeed, the physical restoration of Jesus from the grave does such violence to the previously inexorable logic of the "atonement" theory, that one wonders if, by that resurrection act, everything has not been undone which, at so great cost, had seemed to be achieved. It not only does not require Jesus' resurrection from the tomb to complete the doctrine of the "atonement"; but that final event annuls the "atonement"—if it is to be logically correct.

Any way considered, the conventional view of the "atonement" raises more questions than it answers, in the mind of a man who is unable to accept this doctrine by virtue of the "authority" of the ancient Church. That God should have permitted Himself to become entangled in a predicament from which He cannot extricate Himself with honor, unless His own favorite child is slain to reëstablish the divine integrity, is an idea singularly unconvincing to anyone desirous of a consistent belief and faith in an omniscient and omnipotent Father.

All of this theology, however, is premised upon Adam's "fall" in the Garden of Eden. When, therefore, any other explanation is offered for the origin of the human race than the ancient legend found in the opening pages of Genesis, the entire "atonement" theory collapses.

It is a mistake for the self-conceded liberal in theology to assume an attitude of impatience toward the good people who attempt to frustrate the teaching of modern science in the schools. In their regard the theory of the "atonement" is too precious to be jeopardized. They have accepted Christ on these terms, and they feel that to let him go as a "redeemer, ran-

soming the race lost in Adam's fall," would be to
relinquish him altogether.

A very great deal depends upon whether one believes
or disbelieves in Adam. Many a casual layman inquires, testily, why there should be all this ill-tempered
and bad-mannered hubbub among alleged Christians
over the problem of humanity's origin. What difference does it make? How can we possibly be affected,
at this late date, by the triumph of any particular theory
of human creation? What matters it, today, whether
one holds to the myth that Jehovah raised up the first
man out of the dust of the ground, or the almost equally
speculative and unproved guess of biology that man
worked his way up out of the slime of some tropical
swamp? But these are not idle questions! So much
depends upon what theory of man's origin is to receive
the general credence of Christians, that it is no exag-
geration to say that the Christianity of the future will
be molded on a new wheel! Take Adam out of the
theological scheme, and the whole of it demands
reappraisal.

According to the older theology, Christ's mission
to the world is to make right what Adam had made
wrong. If, then, it comes to be believed that there
never was an Adam, must not Christ's life be interpreted on vastly different grounds than were postulated
to explain him throughout the ages of Christianity,
until comparatively recent times?

It may be assumed that belief in the Adam story will

be quite generally relinquished in the near future. Modern education will see to that. Let the conservative pound his pulpit as vigorously as he likes; let the state legislatures resolve to curb the teaching of scientific speculations in the schools; the trend is toward an acceptance of the new hypotheses. At present, the only sector of the old theological wall which the conservatives have put under strong guard is that point where anthropology has laid a siege. And if science rested its new claims solely upon its guess that mankind had developed slowly from a lower form of life, there would be but a slim chance of its winning the favor of persons who would rather hold to doctrines reinforced by ages of pious and sincere faith, in preference to unproved conjectures, based upon frail and incomplete testimony and offered by people more concerned with a mechanistic view of the universe than a teleological explanation postulating a beneficent God with a sublime plan for the spiritual salvation of His creatures.

But the case does not reside exclusively in the custody of the anthropologists. Geology has had somewhat to say on the general subject of world creation, offering certain tangible properties in evidence which are calculated to stagger and silence the opposition. Indeed, every advancement made in the field of the natural sciences makes the Adamic legend less tenable. It will not be long before a man who believes in the Adam story, literally, will be considered an eccentric.

Seeing, then, that this reappraisal of Jesus' work in

the world is due and obviously inevitable, why not make it now? If we are disposed to wonder whether, as many have thought, the Christian Church can survive an abandonment of the orthodox "atonement" theory, perhaps it is better we should begin making the necessary readjustments in our thought concerning Jesus before "the solid rock on which I stand" proves to be but frail rushes under our feet. We must be entirely sympathetic with the conservative in his well-meant endeavor to dispose of the new scientific teaching before it has completely undermined the traditional view of Jesus' sacrificial value to the world. We invite him to be as considerate of us who hope to reappraise the value of Jesus to the world slightly in advance of the hour when the valorous conservative shall have irretrievably lost his case; for he is due to lose it, and that right early.

For the sake of argument, then, let us say that the Adam story as reported in Genesis, believed by the prophets, traduced to the Church, and enshrined in conventional theology, is insupportable. If that assumption be correct, then every corollary of that Adam story, and all the dogmatics premised upon it, including the "atonement" theory, is not only unjustifiable, but a distinct obstacle in the way of a correct view of Christ's mission among men; for if the "atonement" theory be not a valuable asset, it at once becomes an expensive liability.

That much cleared away, we start our thinking about

the Master with all thought of a debt-paying errand deleted from our program. Jesus has come to express the will of God in respect to adequate human living. He has not come primarily to die, but to live. He is here to teach the principles of eternal life—not meaning merely the price one must pay, in fineness of character, sturdiness of faith, and nobility of conduct, as the condition of entering upon another phase of life elsewhere; but an eternal life here and now, to be continued in the beyond.

One wonders what, exactly, has been the peculiar grip upon the imagination and the faith of believers, or what high satisfaction they have had in the thought that Jesus was here to lift a mortgage, so to speak, which The Absolute held upon the human race. If the mission be held to be in the interest of "justice," what is to be said of the justice which regarded with disfavor and mere tolerance whole ages of men who surely were not responsible for their being in the world at all, much less to be resting under an ancient curse imposed upon a remote progenitor, and not to be raised until final payment of the debt was made?

How much more in accord with our natural thought of a beneficent spiritual Father that He should be communicating His wishes for the welfare of His children, as rapidly and freely as they could understand and utilize these disclosures of divine secrets and, "in the fullness of time," endow a favored Son with a communicable wisdom guaranteed to bring happiness and peace through the practice of a universal brotherhood and the enjoyment of a complete fearlessness of every foe except the forces that menace the soul.

In this picture of Jesus he is to be viewed as an eternal character, living the eternal life, and urging others to live it, too. To the achievement of that high spiritual ambition, premised upon a divine Fatherhood which necessarily involved a human brotherhood, every form of social injustice must give way. If, to enjoy the benefits of sonship, we are to concede a universal brotherhood among men, we must treat all persons, everywhere, as our brothers, or relinquish our relation to God as our Father. There was nothing very complicated about this doctrine, but it permitted no trifling. Either a man laid claim to his own divine sonship, with all the rights and privileges thereto pertaining, or he did not; and his sole certification of his choice—whether he would consider himself as God's child and live the eternal life, or disavow that relationship and its supreme benefits—would be manifested in the attitude he maintained toward all other people. If they were his brothers, he was a child of the Highest. They became his brothers only when and if he treated them as brothers. This is the center and circumference of the Christ ideal. His mission to the earth was to teach that principle.

Naturally, all the people of his time who were entirely content with a social order in which they themselves had everything they wanted, and did not relish the idea of a spiritual commonwealth in which altruism, if it were to work effectually, would redistribute certain privileges, were violently opposed to such teaching. Jesus was a disturber of the peace, they said. And when, at length, his ministry had evoked enough interest among the common people to excite the quite justifiable fears of the old institutions that any further talk about brotherhood would jeopardize them, Jesus was given a hasty trial, a brutal execution, and an entombment under cover of night.

Under the stiff and angular logic of the "atonement" theory, Jesus should remain in that tomb. If he had come expressly to die, as Adam would have died, he would better stay dead, as Adam would have stayed dead. Objection may be made that this statement is not as reverent as it ought to be; but how else shall one say it, if it is said at all? And should it not be said?

Under the new interpretation, however, Jesus has not come to die, but to live that he may teach the fact of the eternal life. True, he finds that the full development of his divine discovery about life demands a ministry which eventually takes him to a cross, where he dies the death of a martyr to his cause; but he realizes, while *en route* to Calvary, that his soul is in the hands of a Father abundantly able to insure against his destruction. Wicked men may mangle his body, and so cruelly mistreat it that it ceases to function; but the death of his body only effects the release of his soul.

To all outward seeming, he is dead. In actual fact, he is continuing to live the eternal life. Now, what is the next step in this new interpretation of Jesus' status? His body, broken and bleeding, is useless. His spirit, triumphant and undamaged, has survived. Kind friends take the body and lay it in a tomb. The tomb is sealed. What next? Shall Jesus consider it imperative to his teaching that there is an eternal life, to reveal himself to his disciples who were to become directly responsible for the spread of this message of the soul's survival?

If no final word is spoken, if no assurance is given, if Jesus leaves his torn body on the cross and disappears completely, who shall ever be able to say, with a feeling of certitude, that he lives, or that, because he lives, we shall live also?

Is not the reappearance of Jesus an inevitable requisite to his ministry? Or is it? Can humanity be depended upon to have the necessary faith and spiritual discernment to take Jesus at his word, without this practical, ocular substantiation? What shall we think about that?

Has Jesus disclosed enough truth, in his daily message concerning "eternal living," to make this post-mortem appearance unimportant? Will his reappearance improve the proper functioning of men's faith, or merely dilute it with materialism? Let us have a glimpse at the story and see whether it may shed some light on this problem.

III

All the gospels tell the tale, no two of them in the same way. The discrepancies are many and serious. They are so serious that all of these narratives are automatically relieved of any charge that they might be willfully untrue. A group of witnesses telling widely different tales may have their testimony discredited on the ground that their knowledge of the event to which they testified was inadequate or irrelevant; but they will not be indicted in the charge of having conspired to commit perjury. The gospel writers may have relied too heavily upon the reports they heard of Jesus' resurrection; but, at all events, they are not lying. Their accounts are too widely different to permit of such a thought in the mind of any honest inquirer, no matter how doubtful he might be of the main allegation.

It may be assumed that anyone whose eye is likely to travel over the pages of this chapter is conversant with the resurrection narratives. Consequently, we need not spend much time reviewing them. It will be recalled that Joseph of Arimathea and Nicodemus secure Pilate's permission to entomb the body in Joseph's family sepulcher, newly built and unoccupied.

According to Matthew, some stirring events had immediately followed Jesus' death. The veil of the temple was torn in two; there was an earthquake; old graves opened in the city cemeteries and the bodies of saints long since dead walked the streets. Mark and

Luke mention the rent veil in the temple, but fail to record the restoration of the saints. John is silent on these matters. One may be permitted to suppose that an event so astounding as the spectacle of men long dead now walking about in Jerusalem would be considered worthy of mention by more than one chronicler out of a possible four. We assume this episode in Matthew's account to be legendary.

Matthew says that "on the morrow" (presumably Saturday) the chief priests and Pharisees requested Pilate to set a guard about the tomb, saying, "That deceiver said, while he was yet alive, 'After three days I rise again.' Command therefore that the sepulcher be made sure, until the third day, lest haply his disciples come and steal him away, and say unto the people, 'He is risen from the dead': and the last error will be worse than the first." The guard was set as ordered. Neither Mark, Luke, nor John know about the priests' interview with Pilate or the establishment of the guard about the tomb.

Matthew says that the soldiers came later into the city, reporting Jesus' resurrection, and were given "much money" to spread the report that the body had been stolen by the disciples while they slept. "So they took the money, and did as they were taught; and this saying was spread abroad among the Jews, and continueth until this day." The other gospels know nothing of this matter, though one has a right to believe that, if true, it was of tremendous importance to the early Church to have this fact made known. We may assume that this episode reported by Matthew is also legendary.

Matthew says that on the evening of the Sabbath (Saturday) Mary Magdalene and the other Mary (thought to be the mother of James and Jesus) came to see the sepulcher. There was an earthquake. An angel of the Lord descended from heaven, rolled away the stone, and sat upon it. The guard was terrified "and became as dead men." The angel told the women not to fear; Jesus had risen; they were to inform the disciples of that fact and bid them meet Jesus in Galilee.

Mark brings Mary Magdalene, the other Mary, and Salome to the tomb at sunrise on the first day of the week. They had brought spices for the anointing of the body. Obviously they knew nothing of a sealed tomb or a guard, for they expected to effect an entrance. As they went, they wondered how they should roll away the heavy stone. Arriving, they found the stone rolled away. Entering the tomb, "they saw a young man sitting on the right side, in a white robe; and were amazed." He conveyed much the same message reported in Matthew of the angel. The women "went out, and fled from the tomb; for trembling and astonishment had come upon them; and they said nothing to any one; for they were afraid."

Luke reports that at early dawn Mary Magdalene, the other Mary, Joanna, and some unnamed women came to the tomb with spices, found the stone rolled away, entered, and it was empty. Two men, in dazzling apparel, appeared, calmed their fears, and reminded them of Jesus' prediction that he would rise from the dead. There was no instruction given them, however, concerning a message to be relayed to the disciples. The women reported their experience to the apostles, however; "and these words appeared in their sight as idle talk; and they disbelieved them."

Peter went hurriedly to the sepulcher, notwithstanding the general incredulity of the apostles, looked in, saw the linen clothes, "and departed to his home, wondering at that which was come to pass."

John says that Mary Magdalene went alone to the tomb while it was yet dark on the morning of the first day of the week. Finding the stone removed, she hurried away, located Peter and John, reported the Master's body gone, "and we know not where they have laid him." ("We" implies that Mary may have been accompanied by some person whom John omits to mention.) It will be well to bear it in mind that we are presumably having the story now from an eyewitness. Peter and John run to the tomb, the latter arriving first. Both enter, see the discarded graveclothes, "and believed." An interesting sentence follows: "For as yet they knew not the scripture that he must rise again from the dead." If Peter and John were unaware of this prediction of the resurrection, to whom, indeed, would such information have been vouchsafed? "They knew not the *scripture!" What* scripture? Peter and John do not tarry. "The disciples went away again unto their own home."

At this point the narrative in John becomes of extraordinary beauty. Mary Magdalene has been standing outside the sepulcher, weeping. Upon the departure of the two disciples she enters the tomb, and finds two angels in white, sitting at either end of the crypt. They inquire why she weeps. She explains. Some one has taken away her Lord. The angels offer no suggestions. Turning back, and now presumably outside the tomb, she saw a man standing whom she mistook for the gardener. She repeats her query: "Sir, if thou hast borne him hence, tell me where thou hast laid him, and I will take him away."

Here we have an excellent example of the Johannine treatment, previously reviewed at considerable length. The same sustainment of dramatic interest, observable in so many of the narratives in this document, postpones Mary's recognition. To achieve that end, John makes Mary inquire of the gardener whether he had taken away the body (an extremely unlikely probability), and, if so, she would like to know where it is, "and I will take him away." One mentions this dilemma solely to point out that we are not expected to take this conversation as literally exact. Mary Magdalene was not likely to take with her the corpse of her Master, even if the gardener was able to lead her to it.

Jesus now reveals himself in the tone with which

he speaks her name. It is implied that she made some gesture of affectionate approach. He warned her. "Touch me not; for I am not yet ascended unto the Father: but go unto my brethren and say to them, I ascend unto my Father and your Father, and my God and your God."

It should be kept in mind that John and Peter have but lately left the garden of the sepulcher. Jesus sends the message to them through Mary Magdalene, though the responsibility for the spread of the gospel, in the coming days, depended so very considerably more upon these men than upon Mary. Why this apparent reluctance of Jesus to deal directly with these men when, that night, he seeks them in their assembly room?

He passes through closed doors that night and appears to the disciples, exhibits his wounded hands and side, and declares, "Whosoever sins ye forgive, they are forgiven unto them; whosoever ye retain, they are retained." It may be suspected that this is a later interpolation, for it is entirely inconsistent with the teachings of Jesus concerning the direct access of the believer to God, in prayer. We have no record that John was ever in Rome, and one cannot conceive of these words having been written elsewhere.

A week later Jesus again appears, according to John. Thomas, doubtful of his vision, is requested to put his fingers into Jesus' wounds, which he does, and is convinced. John intimates that there were other events confirmatory of Jesus' resurrection, "which are not written in this book."

Afterward (the interval not indicated) "Jesus manifested himself again to the disciples at the sea of Tiberius." This is the only time in any gospel record that the sea of Galilee is called the sea of Tiberius. The latter name must have been particularly objectionable to the Jews because it was the Roman name for the lake. We are permitted to draw the conclusion that this part of the narrative was of another authorship than John's. In this episode Jesus appears on the beach, calls to the disciples who are unsuccessfully fishing, instructs them where to cast the net, and when the disciples come in he eats with them.

Luke reports that two friends of Jesus, walking toward a suburb of Jerusalem, on the late afternoon of the day of the resurrection, were overtaken by a stranger who conversed freely with them about the reported event, and sat down with them to supper, but vanished from their sight. They hurried to the disciples' assembly room, reported their experience, and were present when Jesus entered the group. According to this account, Jesus said, "See my hands and my feet, that it is I, myself; for a spirit hath not flesh and bones, as ye behold me having." To substantiate his claim, he called for food, and ate it. Then he led them out to the vicinity of Bethany, blessed them, and disappeared into heaven.

Commenting on this incident which Luke handles

more in detail, Mark says, "After these things he was manifested in another form unto two of them, as they walked, on their way into the country. And they went away and told it unto the rest: neither believed they them. Afterward, he was manifested unto the eleven as they sat at meat; and he upbraided them with their unbelief and hardness of heart because they believed not them that had seen him after he was risen." At the close of this interview, "Jesus was received up into heaven."

Matthew takes the disciples into Galilee, "unto the mountain where Jesus had appointed them." There they saw him. Some worshiped; some doubted. No reference is made to an ascension into heaven.

IV

When the American patriot visits the home city of Abraham Lincoln he is shown many a relic loyally treasured by the people of Springfield. On the stone carriage block before the homestead of the great emancipator the word LINCOLN is carved in deep letters. "Was it there in Lincoln's time?" inquires the visitor. The guide is doubtful; thinks it may have been put there later. But there is no question about this being the Lincoln home.

Upon entering the house, one is shown the old hair-cloth davenport and chairs, undoubtedly of the Lincoln period. The pictures on the walls belong to the eighteen-sixties. In the library, an old bookcase is filled with books of the time. One asks the guide, "Did all these things belong to Lincoln?" Somewhat reluctantly the guide replies, "Some of them, no doubt."

"This old davenport, for instance," persists the tourist. "Was this Lincoln's?" The guide answers, "Well, as a matter of actual fact, no. It is said to have been the property of the Edwards family—Mr. Lincoln's law partner, you know. But, as you can see, it belongs to the period; so it was put here to help reconstruct a typical scene of a first-class home in the 'sixties."

"And the pictures?" inquires the visitor.

"We're not sure about all of them," responds the guide. "Some of them may have been here when the Lincolns lived in this house."

"But you don't know which ones?"

"No; and it is reasonably certain that nobody else does."

"And the bookcase. Was that Lincoln's?" The guide is not sure.

One departs from the house with one's faith in the authenticity of the furniture somewhat altered. One is no longer a "fundamentalist" in respect to the old books and pictures, but one's veneration need not be lessened in the slightest degree for the essential Lincoln who, in an hour of crisis, saved the Union. Surely he would be a very superficial thinker and a frail patriot who would let the doubtful authenticity of an old hair-cloth davenport obstruct his view of the nobility of a great hero!

Let the visitor go now to the cemetery and view the Lincoln tomb. As he stands at the grilled iron door and looks reverently upon the huge sarcophagus surrounded by requial emblems, he may find himself saying aloud, "So there lies the body of Lincoln!"

And the guide clears his throat, seems to be on the point of making an explanation, and, when properly encouraged to offer his comments, remarks, "Well, no; Mr. Lincoln's body does not lie there. Many years ago an effort was made by vandals to steal the body. The attempted sacrilege was discovered when this sarcophagus was halfway through the door. You can see the ragged nick in the side of it, there. See? To insure against such a calamity in the future, the trustees buried the body ten feet deep in concrete, beneath this stone floor, and replaced the sarcophagus in its former position. It is empty."

But, even in the face of all this, the patriotic tourist has no right to conclude that a willful deception is going on in Springfield, a conspiracy to make the American public believe things about Lincoln which are not true.

The only worry the patriot need have as he uncovers these minor differences between the way things seem and the way things are, at the Lincoln shrine, is his self-inspecting mood of inquiry as to his own ability to invest what little he himself has, of honor and valor, in the cause of his country's welfare. Whether Lincoln's body is in the sarcophagus, or ten feet deep in concrete, is a minor question. Whether the tourist has learned something about nobility while standing in that hallowed spot, is a major question!

Only sixty years have passed since the people of Springfield resolved to collect and preserve the memorabilia of this great citizen. But even in these sixty years memory has slipped; eyewitnesses have died; conflicting stories have been told—until nobody knows, certainly, whether there is anything in the old Lincoln home that actually belonged to Lincoln, except possibly the dining table and two chairs; and there is no hard and fast proof about *them*. If sixty years could work such strange tricks with a great man's relics, what is to be said about the minor details of a story *thirty-three times older?* Is Lincoln a myth, if it turns out that the old davenport belonged to the Edwards family? Did Lincoln never live, if it is proved that the pictures on the walls of the homestead were the property of some friendly neighbor? Does it disprove Jesus' survival, as a living spirit of life and leading, if Mark says there was one angel at the tomb, while Luke reports the presence of two angels? Or, if it should be disproved that there were any angels at all, will that annul the eternal leadership of Christ?

One pleasant feature of this bewildering maze of conflicting statements is that the Christian is left practically free to consult his own heart for an opinion of the manner of the Master's survival. He cannot say, with any assurance, that Matthew knows more about it than Luke, or that John may be presumed (as an eye-witness at the tomb) to be more conversant with the fact than Mark (whose gospel antedates all the others). What is left for one to think about all this, in view of the general tangle of evidence?

It has frequently been pointed out that the radical change in the disciples themselves indicates that something had happened to transform them from a group of timid, frail-faithed fishermen, into valorous adventurers. It is difficult to deduce this clearly from the narratives. One is rather disposed to believe that the impression gradually deepens in their minds that their Lord has survived, becoming more and more confident of his spiritual presence, and increasingly emboldened by the remembered inspiration of his fearlessness.

The fact remains—no matter how one decides the change in them was wrought, or exactly when—that the disciples start forth on a death-defying campaign of teaching Christ's gospel, the essential value of which they premise upon their sure belief that they were confident of Jesus' survival. They said he was still alive! Whatever the processes by which he came alive, they knew he was alive! *He was alive!* When we review the strange history of Christianity in the world: how, through the ages, it has grown more and more powerful in its influence; how, at this present hour, more people are confessing their love for and belief in the Man of Galilee, than ever before—we may be assured that, whatever was the manner of his survival, he survived. *No dead Christ could have done it!*

V

Somewhat belatedly, for this is not a matter which one may rush through with impetuous haste, we listen for the "overtones" in this strange minstrelsy that sings of an eternal Christ. The orthodox religion wants Jesus to be sealed in the tomb. The political state is no less eager to make fast the door of the sepulcher. Jesus is dead: let him stay dead. Caiaphas may have his misgivings over the murder, and his own part in it. He intimates that he is not proud of his achievement. Now and again a man has to be sacrificed for the people: that was implied by one narrator as the attitude of Caiaphas. He wants the tomb sealed, lest the disciples steal the body, report a resurrection, and "the last error be worse than the first." So there had been an error, then! Of course; Caiaphas was sorry. But, now that it was all over, Jesus must stay dead. Pilate was sorry, too. He knew Jesus to be innocent; pleaded for his release; refused to humor the priests when they found the inscription on the cross "The King of the Jews" a bit too subtle for so dull a crowd; cheerfully acceded to the request of Joseph and Nicodemus that the body be given into their care. Certainly, Pilate was sorry: but it was better, from the standpoint of the state, that Jesus remain in the tomb.

The disciples are not quite sure, at first, whether to trust their own sight. They have times when they are entirely convinced. He comes to them through closed doors, eats a fish in their presence, invites them to handle his wounds, but up in Galilee, on the mountain where he met them by appointment, some doubted. Not much wonder.

We have hours when we know that survival simply has to be true! The incompleteness of life, without persistence in another world, to explain all this pain, sacrifice, and sorrow! Again we have hours when the utter futility of believing in an immortal life, in the face of the general dissolution and decay of all forms of life, once they have passed fruition, surges over us in a veritable tidal wave of incredulity! We cast about for philosophical substantiations of our hope, but without very much reward. Some Christian advocate delights us momentarily, on Easter, by reminding us that every tissue and cell of the body is completely changed and supplanted by other tissues and cells, once in a cycle of seven years. The man who has completed his traditional span of threescore and ten has put down ten outworn bodies. He did not regret the loss of the third or the fifth; why should he lament the disintegration of the tenth? He survived the disposal of the ninth; why should he be less capable of outliving this last body? Oh yes, these thoughts are temporarily soothing to the disturbed mind, but, after all, they do not count for much when one turns the light on them. An elephant that has not been living the eternal life at all, unconcerned, we presume, about his survival spiritually in another world, has been the same elephant through all the anatomical changes which may have given him a half-dozen successive bodies. There is no help in that quarter.

Every frail little analogy attempted in defense of the eternal life proves unable to endure the light of honest investigation. Of course, if people are so eager for proofs that they refuse to examine more of an alleged case in point than such features of it as minister to their hope, and are content to fool themselves with specious arguments, let them humor themselves to the top of their bent, and good luck to them in their endeavors. They are happier than we are, who must scrutinize our facts, cold-bloodedly, or distrust them.

No; we are finally driven back to the elemental simplicity of the Christ culture. He said we were to live the eternal life now and here. We are to achieve that eternal life through oneness with God. He is our Father and we are His children. We become aware of that bond by making practical our belief in it. If He is our Father, all men are our brothers. We demonstrate our faith in that relationship when we enter into this brotherhood, and accept its claims upon us as the driving motive of our every thought, act, and ambition! People who live by that urge live the eternal life! They live as becomes sons of God! The closer they sense this relationship, the less they have to fear. The prospect of putting down an outworn body does not terrorize them; for they are safe in their Father's hands. What He may choose to do to and for their souls, in some other experience, they do not know and need not know. If it is faith that feeds a soul and makes it strong, why should anyone desire to dilute the food on which his soul is nourished by adding to it strange tinctures of materialistic confirmations, intended to improve the flavor? If he lives his eternal life by faith, let him exercise his faith.

You can gather up all the feeble testimonies to which you have access, seemingly pointing materialistically to personal survival in a world beyond; but no one of them will reach on through to your ultimate destination. The fact that you have what certain well-meaning people have called "a mass of cumulative evidence" is of no consequence. There may be so many as forty bridges on a river, each lacking but a span or two of reaching the other side: you are as incapable of a crossing as if there were but one inadequate bridge. "Cumulative" testimony is valueless in this dilemma. Take your eternal life on faith, or disavow it altogether. Philosophy is helpless to aid you, and science knows nothing about it at all. Spiritualism turns out to be a sad disappointment, and its alleged contacts with another world are so grotesque that one's very grief is made jest of by neurasthenics whose "psychic powers" were better exhibited to an alienist than a mourner. The way to Endor is a sad path indeed.

Frequently ardent Christians feel disturbed because many persons lack a definite assurance that they are to live on everlastingly. For many people, eternal life is viewed not as a promise, but as a threat! They have felt the impulse to develop their souls, and have not obeyed it. It is imperative to their peace of mind that they stay where the racket will drown the inner voice. They secure seats close to the jazz orchestra; they must fill every waking moment with distracting sights and sounds. Go to them with the promise of survival in a world where only souls matter, and see whether they like the idea. If they could be definitely assured that, after death, they might sleep sixteen hours more per day than they do now, they would regard the prospect with a sense of relief. They are not living the eternal life here, and they do not look forward pleasurably to living the eternal life elsewhere. We have been quite mistaken in our thought that every man desires to go to heaven. For many people the thought of survival in a spiritual world where they would be unable to carry along the material possessions which, in this world, have been their entire reliance and exclusive interest, is intolerable.

VI

Unquestionably the most delightful and reassuring of all the resurrection legends is the experience of Mary

Magdalene in the garden of the sepulcher. Mary has hurried to the tomb, at dawn, to minister to the dead body of her Master. After a brief glance into the empty tomb she looks about, outside, for some one of whom she may make inquiry.

Among the flowers—(for our imagination is as useful as anyone's)—bending over the flowers, in the garden, was a man, presumably the gardener; and Mary approached to ask where they had taken the body of her friend; and lo—it was he!

Perhaps, if we might see them, we would find our precious dead are not so far removed from us as we had thought. Perhaps they are still interested in flowers and sunshine and green grass and blue sky and spring, or whatever may be the spiritual equivalents of these beautiful things.

Is there, in any literature of love or liturgy of worship, a more stirringly lovely story than this—of a liberated spirit, in such close contact with our common interests that we may mistake him for the gardener as he touches the roses with nail-torn hands, yet so fully in the confidence of The Absolute that he can guarantee us eternal life, in his name?

One presumes that some reader will say, "Sentiment!" We plead guilty. Unquestionably, that is what it is. There seems to be quite a bit of it interlaced with any satisfying thought about the eternal life. Indeed, it is to be doubted if one can live the eternal life, here at least, without it.

I realize, as I come to the end of this chapter, that I have dealt with my theme mostly in a mood of inquiry, merely making my own questions articulate and declaring very little of sure knowledge about it. Some may say it were better to have thought through this problem a little farther before presuming to talk about it at all to other people.

In reply, I suggest that you summon the wisest, most faith-filled, most self-confident prophet you know, and bring him into our conference, now that we have talked it over; and after he has told us all about immortality, and the world beyond, we shall inquire of him, "What makes you talk so glibly about death? *You* never died!"

CHAPTER TWELVE

GREATER WORKS THAN THESE

I

NOW that we have made a sketchy review of a group of typical miracle stories, with intent to learn what lessons are implied by them of practical availment to us, the question naturally arises: To what degree and extent may our contemporaneous Christian order presume to attempt the solution of its problems by invoking divine assistance?

It may be suspected that the reader, if a Christian in faith and practice, will immediately find in his own observation and experience a ready answer to this query; for he has full confidence in the power of prayer. For ages, he says, men of all faiths have been calling upon Deity for aid with an assurance certifying to the reality and practicableness of such supplication. To his mind, our question seems easily answered.

The salutary uses of prayer may be promptly conceded, however, without solving the problem before us. What we want to know is: Can a Christian of our own day successfully invoke the same type of divine power employed by the Master? Our inquiry roots itself in the problem: When Jesus said of his deeds, *"The works that I do shall ye do also, and greater works than these shall ye do,"* exactly what did he mean? It is high time we found out! If there is accessible to us a vast field of undeveloped and unclaimed divine energy awaiting a rediscovery by faith, we should accept our legacy and thereby enrich ourselves.

There is plenty of warrant, in the reported sayings of Jesus, for our belief that his alleged supernormal works might and could be wrought by others than himself, provided they brought to the projected task an adequate faith. According to a statement predicated of Jesus, mountains could be removed by the exercise of a faith so diminutive as a grain of mustard seed.

Some have tried to reduce the difficulties involved in that declaration by suggesting that Jesus referred to the latent power for tremendous expansion and development resident in the mustard seed, rather than to the small size of it. One doubts if that exposition is correct. An investigation of the sources indicates that Jesus used the mustard seed as an illustration because it was dimensionally insignificant. It was as if one might say, "If you had *a penny's worth of faith,* you could perform miracles with it!"

Is it possible for us to possess ourselves of a faith potent enough to accomplish feats for which we have no natural capacity? If it is impossible to arrive at that type of faith, any promise of divine power as a reward of such faith is purely hypothetical, in which case the problem resolves itself into a mere academic riddle with no outcome in human experience. Roughly stated, the logic of the situation runs, rather depressingly, as follows: Jesus said, "If ye have faith as a grain of mustard seed, ye shall say unto this mountain, 'Remove hence to yonder place,' and it shall remove." But no mountain has ever been removed by faith; therefore it may be held that no man has ever laid hold upon the type of faith sufficient for such an achievement. Christianity has been at work for more than nineteen centuries, and no mountains removed to this date.

At this juncture, however, some one rises to declare that mountains have been removed, and cites facts to show that faith motivated these undertakings. We are advised to consider the Panama Canal as a striking example of the removal of mountains. It may pay us to investigate this and see if it is a case in point.

II

When Columbus returned to Spain from the voyage which was distinguished by his discovery of a new Western World, he was obliged to admit to his financial sponsors that he had failed to accomplish the mission on which he had been sent. The fact that he had found an unmapped continent was quite beside the point. He had gone forth seeking a western passage from Europe to Cathay, and had not found it. However his promoters may have been casually interested in the discovery of the untamed and untilled Americas, they were as eager as before to find an easier route to the rich and well-developed markets of remote countries where ages of commercial progress and experience had produced mobile wealth.

Columbus reported that the Americas constituted a barrier to that contemplated westerly passage, but that a narrow isthmus, uniting these huge countries, might possibly be opened. At once the question of a ship canal was at issue. Within a few years, a technical book had been written on the subject by a Portuguese engineer, and an eminent Spanish statesman had urged Philip II to undertake the work without delay. These facts are mentioned merely to indicate the length of time—three and a half centuries—which elapsed between the conception and the consummation of this task.

For an extended period, whatever work was done on the removal of the mountains which barred the way across the isthmus was confined to books, tracts, and debates around council tables. Surveying parties went to the strategic zone from Spain, Portugal, Holland, Belgium, England and France, returning to wrangle over the problem of the best route across the barrier, strikingly reminding one of the wordy theological controversies staged, from time immemorial, over "the only way" to reach our desired haven.

So the polemic warfare went on among the headstrong and contentious engineers, each loudly declaring the remarkable rightness of his own blueprints and endeavoring to show up his professional brethren as a group of unskilled and untrustworthy nobodies. But no amount of squabbling over whether the best way across the American isthmus was by Nicaragua, Panama, San Blas, Caledonia Bay, Darien, or the Atrato River had turned a single shovelful of dirt or decreased the time and distance between Europe and Cathay by a minute or a mile! The sum total of results, so far, was the engendering of much bitter strife and the complete disappointment of the mercantile interests, who were not so greatly concerned about the best way to cross the isthmus as for almost any kind of a way that would meet the requirements of their ships.

At length the heat of controversy cooled sufficiently to permit one hundred and thirty-five representatives of the interested countries to convene, without too much danger of doing one another physical damage, and at that conference in Paris it was resolved to place the whole enterprise in the hands of Ferdinand de Lesseps. It now began to look as if the movement held out some promise of success. For three hundred and twenty-nine years nothing had been accomplished but talk. An enormous sum of money was secured and the resourceful Frenchman set to work. Again and again the gigantic task slowed up for want of funds. More and more money was dumped into the great ditch. At length, when everything that money, zeal, industry and patience could do had proved inadequate, the promoters sadly abandoned the project, left their costly machinery rusting in the yellow mud, and declared the thing impossible.

What made it impossible was the difficulty of securing enough man power to perform the labor. Men could not live down there. They speedily fell ill and were incapacitated. Hosts of them died. Recruits could not be brought into the dangerous area fast enough to fill the depleting ranks. There wasn't enough money in the whole world to solve the problem. So the mountains still stood unremoved which barred the way from Europe to Cathay.

After many years of Western civilization's hopeless resignation to the belief that the canal was an impossibility, our own country paid a large sum of money for the machinery and whatever else was of value in the ditch, including a fair price for the labor already done, and activities were resumed. Our American engineers began their research with a frank admission that the first and gravest problem to be solved was the question of the laborers' health. They conceded that the canal project was not primarily an engineering problem. Pursuant to their belief, they sent for distinguished physicians and gave them the right of way in the Canal Zone. These physicians, upon looking into the nature of the disease which undermined the workmen's health, pronounced it a contagion carried by some insect. Promptly they retired in favor of skilled bacteriologists, even as the engineers had previously retired in favor of the doctors. The bacteriologists were unable to say which of the seventy-four different kinds of mosquitoes were carrying the malaria, and backed off the stage in favor of scientifically trained entomologists. Many startling feats of heroism were performed in those days by these scientists who permitted themselves to be bitten by poisonous insects in an effort to secure the data necessary to their research.

After long and dangerous experimentation, they found the mosquito that had caused the trouble, destroyed its breeding places, screened the laborers' quarters, made the isthmus safe to live on; and the mountains were removed which barred the way of that western passage from Europe to Cathay.

III

When, therefore, some one rises to declare that mountains have been removed by faith, and cites the Panama Canal as a case of it, we cheerfully concede that here is indeed an admirable illustration of faith achieving mighty works—even greater works than were performed by the Master, if one wishes to estimate the relative importance of deeds by the number of foot-pounds lifted or the number of persons immediately benefited.

But here was no "Presto; pass!" type of miracle. To the removal of those isthmian mountains there had to be applied a faith large enough to understand the importance of the task's success as immeasurably greater than any individual's theories or professional rights and dignities.

When all the people interested in the project had become so passionately eager to see it succeed that they would defer to men whom they outranked, by the customary standards, they declared a type of faith that has mountain-moving possibilities.

What a thrilling story it is—this Panama epic—in its capacity to illumine the way for us who wish to know how a kinetic faith may be achieved. How many apparently trifling episodes, occurring decades and leagues away from the scene of this gigantic project, bulk large as they bring their findings to the task of removing the mountains! What a volume of professional pride had to be swallowed by the forward-looking pathologists of Europe when they begged old man Leeuwenhoek, the ignorant and unkempt janitor of the City Hall at Delft, to let them have a peek into his microscope! But that same self-abasement on the part of the wise, who were willing to learn from the simple, if that were the price of knowing the truth, was the exact cost of the prayer which brought the mystery of the subvisible universe under the mastery of mankind!

What a pocketing of professional vanity had to be suffered by the world's mechanical engineers when they accepted the accidental discovery of an indolent boy who, employed to pull the strings which operated the valves of a crude steam engine, was too lazy to do his work, and invented the "eccentric" to do it for him, while he sat by, reading penny thrillers.

What a debauch of self-effacement the electrical wiseacres of the world had to endure when they besought the young bookbinder, Faraday, to teach them how to make a dynamo!

All this had happened long before the removal of the isthmian mountains, but events showed that these valorous self-effacements were necessary steps on the way toward the ultimate performance of the great task. And when, at Panama, the civil engineers stepped back and gave the right of way to the doctors, who immediately retired in favor of the bacteriologists, who promptly sent for the entomologists, it meant that here was the same type of faith at work, believed and practiced by men to whom *the ship was more important than the crew!*

Long before the Panama workers had had a chance to show the depth, breadth, and glory of their self-abandoning sportsmanship, others before them had been "in honor preferring one another." The engines that drove their colossal dredges had been produced by the sort of faith that is more concerned with finding the secret than conserving the dignity of the seeker. The gigantic electrical machinery had been evolved through the self-forgetting courage of great men to whom the quest was more important than the explorer. The microscope, and the whole related business of investigating the microcosmic world, had come in on the wings of a self-renouncing faith. That is the way mountains are removed! No mountains ever obeyed the commands of people who thought more of their own opinions, their own decrees, their own professional standing, their own assumed superiorities, their own gold lace, embroidered vestments, and brass hats, than they thought of the high importance of seeing the great thing come to pass—somehow, anyhow, just so it came to pass!

Perhaps we have not given quite enough attention to that remark of the astute Tarsan, "Not many wise men, not many mighty, are called . . . but God hath chosen the foolish things of the world to confound the wise . . . and the weak things to confound the great, and base things of the world, and things which are despised hath God chosen . . . that no flesh should glory in His presence." It is as if God said: "How sincerely do you want this thing? Do you want it enough to send your wisest men humbly into the presence of lowly and ignorant people, seeking light of them, as proof of your and their earnestness?"

In other words, a faith that is sufficiently genuine to take complete command of a man's soul, forcing him to waive aside all his inherited prejudices, deny all his dearest preconceptions, forget all his scholastic refinements, all his professional prides and honors, humbly asking counsel of others whom he outranks, by every common standard of comparison; a faith that is so eager to see the world possess this great benefit (whatever it may be) that its possessor will absolutely forget all his own private interests, and, if necessary, actually offer his life as part payment on the cost of the secret—such faith always did and always will remove mountains! Nor can they be removed by any type of faith less capable or less expensive.

IV

Unquestionably, a new day has dawned in the experience of organized Christianity. The new thinking has wrought a disturbing havoc upon the old slogans, the old shibboleths, the old "authority." Protestantism seems to have been rapidly reorganizing into two generic groups, practically independent of the sectarian boundaries hitherto marking the distinctive fields of thought in which the denominations have operated. One group insists that the authority of an infallible Book as interpreted by men who consider it the veritable product of God, must be maintained.

In the long run, this comes to the same type of authority which Romanism vests in the high councils of the Church.

But what do we want with authority in religion, after all's said? There is very little that can be even rhetorically referred to as "authority" anywhere else in life. Why should it be demanded or expected in the field of religion? There is no authority, for example, in the medical profession. That does not mean that the doctors are dishonest, or idle, or useless. The fact that there are many different techniques and opinions reso-lutely believed and practiced by as many different types of doctors does not discredit the profession. The lay-man does not say, "I shall consult no more doctors about my health until all the doctors have agreed, not only in respect to what ails me, but in all other patho-logical matters, as well." And if there should be re-solved, by some smug and well-established medical school, that it was able to speak in tones of finality; if it should say, "All the doctors who disagree with us are numskulls who ought to be barred from practice. We know it all. We not only are making no mistakes, but we cannot make mistakes, for we possess final authority on all therapeutic issues"—if any cultus among physicians should risk such a declaration, one suspects that the only type of patients they could enlist, thereafter, would be the simple-minded souls who, in every generation, make quackery possible and profitable.

No; the doctors continue to learn by experience and research. Their profession is not a static institution, based upon the findings of physicians in the remote past and deduced from venerable parchments. It is, rather, a living, growing quest of knowledge, so eager to lay hold upon fresh facts that it frequently concedes the truth of new hypotheses which automatically make every current textbook on the illumined subject worth just what it will fetch per pound at the paper mill. No authority is wanted in medicine; and whoever insists that he is or has ultimate authority in that field could make no clearer announcement that he is a quack.

Of course, the medical men have staked off a few definite territories in which they walk unifiedly and confidently. They have proved that by the use of a certain vaccine, the scourge of smallpox can be—because it has been—stamped out. We do not vaccinate on the ground that the medical profession has received a divine communication to the effect that vaccination will prevent smallpox, but because we know experimentally that it does. We do not stake our faith in such treatment because physicians say they found the formula in a book which they consider authoritative and held by them to be infallible, but because we have sure evidence that the thing works. That little scar on your arm did not come there because you thought it fitting and in good taste and conformable to current conventionality that you should go through a mysterious ceremony in which some priest in the Temple of Materia Medica made this sign on you, to indicate that you were now of the sacred cult of believers in St. Louis Pasteur, with a side line of devotion to the names of Sts. Jenner, Bradlaugh, Bristowe, Hunter, Savery, and White. Not a bit of it! The scar means that you knew vaccination was a reasonable insurance against a loathsome disease. You accepted it on the strength of what such prophylactic measures had done for other people; and the problem of authority, proceeding from any group of self-confessed wiseacres, never entered your mind.

And what is true of the complete lack of final authority in the field of medicine and surgery is as true in every scientific endeavor to which we look for our physical comfort, light, power, and general education.

Buddhism can make all the extravagant claims it wishes to project, as to the divine authority of its holy scriptures and the leading of its God-begotten chieftain; the fact that it still plows its outworn soil with a crooked stick, still grovels in filth and flies and fleas, still lights its wretched hovel with a smoking grease lamp, still lives on a plane of social equality with its domestic animals, is enough to make any intelligent mind skeptical of its boasts. The only "authority" that any religion can offer is its fruits. You cannot grow figs on a thistle. Will it work?—Has it worked?—Does it work?—that is the ultimate test; and there is no book, no prophet, no alleged divinity able to command respect until and unless that pragmatic inquiry be answered with demonstrable facts.

We have not been trying to show, in this study, that Jesus wrought wonders because he was, biologically considered, the begotten of God. There have been too many other Sons of God, according to various holy books, whose supernatural births were chronicled in terms every way as dramatic and awe-inspiring as the traditional story of Jesus' birth in Bethlehem, for us to ascribe power to him on such grounds. The belief that Jesus rose from the tomb, and revealed himself in physical presence to his disciples, would mean little if we had it to accept or deny on a sheer basis of an intellectual assent or dissent to an article in a creed.

Our claim for Jesus as a worker of wonders rests upon the fact that he is working wonders. Where his gospel goes, the first effect is the freeing of men's minds from untenable superstitions and morbid fears of the unknown. Thus released from their slavery to the hard taskmaster that ignorance always is, they are able to do some constructive thinking; they attempt arts and culture; they look for new means of reducing human ills. By this program of mutual trust and confidence they begin to work coöperatively to the achievement of high aims which no man, single-handedly, can hope to accomplish. Jesus is performing these wonders *now*.

The liberal group of Christians is at work on a reappraisal of the value of Jesus, operating rather from this end of the long journey of Christianity through the ages than the other. We, too, are infatuated with the mystery and essential beauty of the story of Jesus as contained in the gospels, not because we consider them infallible, which we do not, or written by the direct dictation of God, which we do not, but because we realize that the elemental spirit of the Christ they revered is operative in our present life. It is a most amazing thing to pick up a symposium of old tracts, written nearly two millennia ago, and find their authors —untutored country folk with very little experience of the world—reciting deeds, predicated of their Jesus, which are but types of the vast works of healing and social reconstruction, now operating with such kinetic drive that the normal life expectancy has been increased, in Christian countries, by *sixteen years in the past half century!*

It is still more amazing to find these inexperienced and unlettered Galileans predicting that the time would come when the whole world would be brought into subjection to this divine urge which they had seen at work in the life of their Lord. They believed in that ultimate triumph of the Christ ideal, and its healing ministry to the whole world, and documented that belief at an hour when the sum total of professed Christians in the world was a few hundred poor and uninfluential people, meeting by stealth in obscure quarters. When the last and most optimistic of the gospels was written, the greatest leader of Christianity had to make sails to buy his bread. They said that this discovery of life, which Jesus had made, would conquer all the world! No prophecy was ever made involving such a tremendous task or such an extravagant claim. No prophecy was ever made that seemed less likely of fulfillment. In the face of their rags and persecution, the forecast was little short of ridiculous.

If, however, there had been found four documents, clearly originating in the first century, asserting that one Jesus of Nazareth had healed the sick, cast out devils, and relieved all manner of ills, apparently by divine power, and that he had delegated this marvelous capacity to those who followed him and practiced his rule of life, declaring that his process of social rehabilitation in the ages to come would not only be able to do for suffering humanity all that he had done, but more; if there had been found such documents, but none of these things had come to pass, none of his idealism had survived, none of his principles were any longer cherished—then we should have good reason for saying that these ancient writers had been either deceived by their leader or self-deluded by their own imaginations.

But these things have come to pass, as predicted by the Nazarene nearly twenty centuries ago and reported by a handful of fishermen who wrote what they had seen and heard, in books which are only in recent years beginning to be understood at something like face value, as his predictions and his disciples' claims for him come true.

As to the exact nature of the power he exercised and transmitted, the power now motivating our scientized altruism, we would better confess that we do not know, certainly, much about it. We will have to fall back upon the stubborn answer of the blind man in John's remarkable story, who, in reply to all queries, shouted, "I only know that whereas I was blind, now I see!"

We cannot explain the power which, deriving from a single individual, has come plunging along through the ages, bearing a flaming torch, picking up whole nations and races and making them over from savages and cannibals, skulking half-naked in the woods, into high-powered social states, led by men of tremendous mental acumen, wresting the secrets of energy and light from the very hand of God. We only know that whereas they were once blind, now they can see.

We cannot explain how, by laying hold upon the divine friendship of a cross-slain martyr who went to death as a disturber of a decadent orthodoxy in A.D. 28, we today may feel our lives transformed, our minds cleared, our aims repitched, so that we want to invest ourselves in the building of a better world; but we know that this friendship is real. Confidently we make our way by the light of that Galilean torch, even into the deepening shadows of life's inevitable evening, calmly and unafraid. We do not pretend to understand the full mystery of that light, but we know that by its radiance we can see. And if, by that light, the advancing host of civilized men marches daily into larger privilege and better knowledge of the ways which point to a golden age of prosperity founded upon social justice, kindness, and generosity, I can hold, with the full intellectual pride of one critical of facts until they have been adequately verified, to a belief that I may trust that ineffable radiance all the way and into a world beyond.

> "So, if I stoop
>   Into a dark, tremendous sea of cloud,
>   It is but for a time:
>   I press God's lamp close to my breast;

Its splendors, soon or late,
Will pierce the gloom.
I shall emerge, one day."

THE END